MW00885573

This Journal Belongs To:

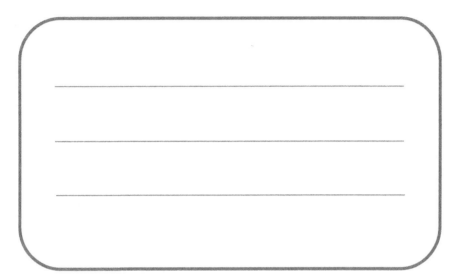

Copyright © 2021
All rights reserved

Notary Information:

FULL NAME: _____

_____

ADDRESS: _____

_____

_____

EMAIL: _____

PHONE NUMBER: _____

FAX NUMBER: _____

NOTES: _____

_____

_____

Log Book Information:

LOG NUMBER: _____

START DATE: _____

END DATE: _____

NOTARY RECORD

FULL NAME:

EMAIL:

THUMB PRINT

PHONE NUMBER:

SIGNER'S SIGNATURE:

ADDRESS:

SERVICES PROVIDED:	IDENTIFICATION:		ID NUMBER:
☐ JURAT	☐ ID CARD	☐ CREDIBLE WITNESS	
☐ OATH	☐ PASSPORT	☐ KNOWN PERSONALLY	ISSUED BY:
☐ ACKNOWLEDGEMENT	☐ DRIVERS LICENSE		DATE ISSUE : / EXPIRATION DATE:
☐ OTHER :	☐ OTHER :		

WITNESS FULL NAME:

EMAIL:

PHONE NUMBER:

WITNESS SIGNATURE:

ADDRESS:

DOCUMENT TYPE:	DATE/TIME NOTARIZED:	DOCUMENT DATE:	FEE CHARGED:

COMMENTS:

RECORD NUMBER: **1**

NOTARY RECORD

FULL NAME:

EMAIL:

THUMB PRINT

PHONE NUMBER:

SIGNER'S SIGNATURE:

ADDRESS:

SERVICES PROVIDED:	IDENTIFICATION:		ID NUMBER:
☐ JURAT	☐ ID CARD	☐ CREDIBLE WITNESS	
☐ OATH	☐ PASSPORT	☐ KNOWN PERSONALLY	ISSUED BY:
☐ ACKNOWLEDGEMENT	☐ DRIVERS LICENSE		DATE ISSUE : / EXPIRATION DATE:
☐ OTHER :	☐ OTHER :		

WITNESS FULL NAME:

EMAIL:

PHONE NUMBER:

WITNESS SIGNATURE:

ADDRESS:

DOCUMENT TYPE:	DATE/TIME NOTARIZED:	DOCUMENT DATE:	FEE CHARGED:

COMMENTS:

RECORD NUMBER: **2**

NOTARY RECORD

FULL NAME:

EMAIL:

THUMB PRINT

PHONE NUMBER:

SIGNER'S SIGNATURE:

ADDRESS:

SERVICES PROVIDED:	IDENTIFICATION:		ID NUMBER:	
☐ JURAT	☐ ID CARD	☐ CREDIBLE WITNESS		
☐ OATH	☐ PASSPORT	☐ KNOWN PERSONALLY	ISSUED BY:	
☐ ACKNOWLEDGEMENT	☐ DRIVERS LICENSE		DATE ISSUE :	EXPIRATION DATE:
☐ OTHER :	☐ OTHER :			

WITNESS FULL NAME:

EMAIL:

PHONE NUMBER:

WITNESS SIGNATURE:

ADDRESS:

DOCUMENT TYPE:	DATE/TIME NOTARIZED:	DOCUMENT DATE:	FEE CHARGED:

COMMENTS:	RECORD NUMBER: 3

NOTARY RECORD

FULL NAME:

EMAIL:

THUMB PRINT

PHONE NUMBER:

SIGNER'S SIGNATURE:

ADDRESS:

SERVICES PROVIDED:	IDENTIFICATION:		ID NUMBER:	
☐ JURAT	☐ ID CARD	☐ CREDIBLE WITNESS		
☐ OATH	☐ PASSPORT	☐ KNOWN PERSONALLY	ISSUED BY:	
☐ ACKNOWLEDGEMENT	☐ DRIVERS LICENSE		DATE ISSUE :	EXPIRATION DATE:
☐ OTHER :	☐ OTHER :			

WITNESS FULL NAME:

EMAIL:

PHONE NUMBER:

WITNESS SIGNATURE:

ADDRESS:

DOCUMENT TYPE:	DATE/TIME NOTARIZED:	DOCUMENT DATE:	FEE CHARGED:

COMMENTS:	RECORD NUMBER: 4

NOTARY RECORD

FULL NAME:	EMAIL:	THUMB PRINT
PHONE NUMBER:	SIGNER'S SIGNATURE:	
ADDRESS:		

SERVICES PROVIDED:	IDENTIFICATION:		ID NUMBER:
☐ JURAT	☐ ID CARD	☐ CREDIBLE WITNESS	
☐ OATH	☐ PASSPORT	☐ KNOWN PERSONALLY	ISSUED BY:
☐ ACKNOWLEDGEMENT	☐ DRIVERS LICENSE		DATE ISSUE : / EXPIRATION DATE:
☐ OTHER :	☐ OTHER :		

WITNESS FULL NAME:	EMAIL:
PHONE NUMBER:	WITNESS SIGNATURE:
ADDRESS:	

DOCUMENT TYPE:	DATE/TIME NOTARIZED:	DOCUMENT DATE:	FEE CHARGED:

COMMENTS:	RECORD NUMBER: 5

NOTARY RECORD

FULL NAME:	EMAIL:	THUMB PRINT
PHONE NUMBER:	SIGNER'S SIGNATURE:	
ADDRESS:		

SERVICES PROVIDED:	IDENTIFICATION:		ID NUMBER:
☐ JURAT	☐ ID CARD	☐ CREDIBLE WITNESS	
☐ OATH	☐ PASSPORT	☐ KNOWN PERSONALLY	ISSUED BY:
☐ ACKNOWLEDGEMENT	☐ DRIVERS LICENSE		DATE ISSUE : / EXPIRATION DATE:
☐ OTHER :	☐ OTHER :		

WITNESS FULL NAME:	EMAIL:
PHONE NUMBER:	WITNESS SIGNATURE:
ADDRESS:	

DOCUMENT TYPE:	DATE/TIME NOTARIZED:	DOCUMENT DATE:	FEE CHARGED:

COMMENTS:	RECORD NUMBER: 6

NOTARY RECORD

FULL NAME:	EMAIL:	THUMB PRINT
PHONE NUMBER:	SIGNER'S SIGNATURE:	
ADDRESS:		

SERVICES PROVIDED:	IDENTIFICATION:		ID NUMBER:
☐ JURAT	☐ ID CARD	☐ CREDIBLE WITNESS	
☐ OATH	☐ PASSPORT	☐ KNOWN PERSONALLY	ISSUED BY:
☐ ACKNOWLEDGEMENT	☐ DRIVERS LICENSE		DATE ISSUE : EXPIRATION DATE:
☐ OTHER :	☐ OTHER :		

WITNESS FULL NAME:	EMAIL:
PHONE NUMBER:	WITNESS SIGNATURE:
ADDRESS:	

DOCUMENT TYPE:	DATE/TIME NOTARIZED:	DOCUMENT DATE:	FEE CHARGED:
COMMENTS:			RECORD NUMBER: 7

NOTARY RECORD

FULL NAME:	EMAIL:	THUMB PRINT
PHONE NUMBER:	SIGNER'S SIGNATURE:	
ADDRESS:		

SERVICES PROVIDED:	IDENTIFICATION:		ID NUMBER:
☐ JURAT	☐ ID CARD	☐ CREDIBLE WITNESS	
☐ OATH	☐ PASSPORT	☐ KNOWN PERSONALLY	ISSUED BY:
☐ ACKNOWLEDGEMENT	☐ DRIVERS LICENSE		DATE ISSUE : EXPIRATION DATE:
☐ OTHER :	☐ OTHER :		

WITNESS FULL NAME:	EMAIL:
PHONE NUMBER:	WITNESS SIGNATURE:
ADDRESS:	

DOCUMENT TYPE:	DATE/TIME NOTARIZED:	DOCUMENT DATE:	FEE CHARGED:
COMMENTS:			RECORD NUMBER: 8

NOTARY RECORD

FULL NAME:

EMAIL:

THUMB PRINT

PHONE NUMBER:

SIGNER'S SIGNATURE:

ADDRESS:

SERVICES PROVIDED:	IDENTIFICATION:		
☐ JURAT	☐ ID CARD	☐ CREDIBLE WITNESS	**ID NUMBER:**
☐ OATH	☐ PASSPORT	☐ KNOWN PERSONALLY	**ISSUED BY:**
☐ ACKNOWLEDGEMENT	☐ DRIVERS LICENSE		**DATE ISSUE :**
☐ OTHER :	☐ OTHER :		**EXPIRATION DATE:**

WITNESS FULL NAME:

EMAIL:

PHONE NUMBER:

WITNESS SIGNATURE:

ADDRESS:

DOCUMENT TYPE:	DATE/TIME NOTARIZED:	DOCUMENT DATE:	FEE CHARGED:

COMMENTS:

RECORD NUMBER: **9**

NOTARY RECORD

FULL NAME:

EMAIL:

THUMB PRINT

PHONE NUMBER:

SIGNER'S SIGNATURE:

ADDRESS:

SERVICES PROVIDED:	IDENTIFICATION:		
☐ JURAT	☐ ID CARD	☐ CREDIBLE WITNESS	**ID NUMBER:**
☐ OATH	☐ PASSPORT	☐ KNOWN PERSONALLY	**ISSUED BY:**
☐ ACKNOWLEDGEMENT	☐ DRIVERS LICENSE		**DATE ISSUE :**
☐ OTHER :	☐ OTHER :		**EXPIRATION DATE:**

WITNESS FULL NAME:

EMAIL:

PHONE NUMBER:

WITNESS SIGNATURE:

ADDRESS:

DOCUMENT TYPE:	DATE/TIME NOTARIZED:	DOCUMENT DATE:	FEE CHARGED:

COMMENTS:

RECORD NUMBER: **10**

NOTARY RECORD

FULL NAME:	EMAIL:	THUMB PRINT
PHONE NUMBER:	SIGNER'S SIGNATURE:	
ADDRESS:		

SERVICES PROVIDED:	IDENTIFICATION:		ID NUMBER:
☐ JURAT	☐ ID CARD	☐ CREDIBLE WITNESS	
☐ OATH	☐ PASSPORT	☐ KNOWN PERSONALLY	ISSUED BY:
☐ ACKNOWLEDGEMENT	☐ DRIVERS LICENSE		DATE ISSUE : / EXPIRATION DATE:
☐ OTHER :	☐ OTHER :		

WITNESS FULL NAME:	EMAIL:
PHONE NUMBER:	WITNESS SIGNATURE:
ADDRESS:	

DOCUMENT TYPE:	DATE/TIME NOTARIZED:	DOCUMENT DATE:	FEE CHARGED:

COMMENTS:	RECORD NUMBER: 11

NOTARY RECORD

FULL NAME:	EMAIL:	THUMB PRINT
PHONE NUMBER:	SIGNER'S SIGNATURE:	
ADDRESS:		

SERVICES PROVIDED:	IDENTIFICATION:		ID NUMBER:
☐ JURAT	☐ ID CARD	☐ CREDIBLE WITNESS	
☐ OATH	☐ PASSPORT	☐ KNOWN PERSONALLY	ISSUED BY:
☐ ACKNOWLEDGEMENT	☐ DRIVERS LICENSE		DATE ISSUE : / EXPIRATION DATE:
☐ OTHER :	☐ OTHER :		

WITNESS FULL NAME:	EMAIL:
PHONE NUMBER:	WITNESS SIGNATURE:
ADDRESS:	

DOCUMENT TYPE:	DATE/TIME NOTARIZED:	DOCUMENT DATE:	FEE CHARGED:

COMMENTS:	RECORD NUMBER: 12

NOTARY RECORD

FULL NAME:

EMAIL:

THUMB PRINT

PHONE NUMBER:

SIGNER'S SIGNATURE:

ADDRESS:

SERVICES PROVIDED:
- ☐ JURAT
- ☐ OATH
- ☐ ACKNOWLEDGEMENT
- ☐ OTHER : ....

IDENTIFICATION:
- ☐ ID CARD
- ☐ PASSPORT
- ☐ DRIVERS LICENSE
- ☐ OTHER : ....

- ☐ CREDIBLE WITNESS
- ☐ KNOWN PERSONALLY

ID NUMBER:

ISSUED BY:

DATE ISSUE :

EXPIRATION DATE:

WITNESS FULL NAME:

EMAIL:

PHONE NUMBER:

WITNESS SIGNATURE:

ADDRESS:

DOCUMENT TYPE:

DATE/TIME NOTARIZED:

DOCUMENT DATE:

FEE CHARGED:

COMMENTS:

RECORD NUMBER: **13**

NOTARY RECORD

FULL NAME:

EMAIL:

THUMB PRINT

PHONE NUMBER:

SIGNER'S SIGNATURE:

ADDRESS:

SERVICES PROVIDED:
- ☐ JURAT
- ☐ OATH
- ☐ ACKNOWLEDGEMENT
- ☐ OTHER : ....

IDENTIFICATION:
- ☐ ID CARD
- ☐ PASSPORT
- ☐ DRIVERS LICENSE
- ☐ OTHER : ....

- ☐ CREDIBLE WITNESS
- ☐ KNOWN PERSONALLY

ID NUMBER:

ISSUED BY:

DATE ISSUE :

EXPIRATION DATE:

WITNESS FULL NAME:

EMAIL:

PHONE NUMBER:

WITNESS SIGNATURE:

ADDRESS:

DOCUMENT TYPE:

DATE/TIME NOTARIZED:

DOCUMENT DATE:

FEE CHARGED:

COMMENTS:

RECORD NUMBER: **14**

NOTARY RECORD

FULL NAME:	EMAIL:	THUMB PRINT
PHONE NUMBER:	SIGNER'S SIGNATURE:	
ADDRESS:		

SERVICES PROVIDED:	IDENTIFICATION:		ID NUMBER:
☐ JURAT	☐ ID CARD	☐ CREDIBLE WITNESS	
☐ OATH	☐ PASSPORT	☐ KNOWN PERSONALLY	ISSUED BY:
☐ ACKNOWLEDGEMENT	☐ DRIVERS LICENSE		DATE ISSUE : · EXPIRATION DATE:
☐ OTHER :	☐ OTHER :		

WITNESS FULL NAME:	EMAIL:
PHONE NUMBER:	WITNESS SIGNATURE:
ADDRESS:	

DOCUMENT TYPE:	DATE/TIME NOTARIZED:	DOCUMENT DATE:	FEE CHARGED:

COMMENTS:	RECORD NUMBER: **15**

NOTARY RECORD

FULL NAME:	EMAIL:	THUMB PRINT
PHONE NUMBER:	SIGNER'S SIGNATURE:	
ADDRESS:		

SERVICES PROVIDED:	IDENTIFICATION:		ID NUMBER:
☐ JURAT	☐ ID CARD	☐ CREDIBLE WITNESS	
☐ OATH	☐ PASSPORT	☐ KNOWN PERSONALLY	ISSUED BY:
☐ ACKNOWLEDGEMENT	☐ DRIVERS LICENSE		DATE ISSUE : · EXPIRATION DATE:
☐ OTHER :	☐ OTHER :		

WITNESS FULL NAME:	EMAIL:
PHONE NUMBER:	WITNESS SIGNATURE:
ADDRESS:	

DOCUMENT TYPE:	DATE/TIME NOTARIZED:	DOCUMENT DATE:	FEE CHARGED:

COMMENTS:	RECORD NUMBER: **16**

NOTARY RECORD

FULL NAME:

EMAIL:

THUMB PRINT

PHONE NUMBER:

SIGNER'S SIGNATURE:

ADDRESS:

SERVICES PROVIDED:
- ☐ JURAT
- ☐ OATH
- ☐ ACKNOWLEDGEMENT
- ☐ OTHER : ....

IDENTIFICATION:
- ☐ ID CARD
- ☐ PASSPORT
- ☐ DRIVERS LICENSE
- ☐ OTHER : ....

- ☐ CREDIBLE WITNESS
- ☐ KNOWN PERSONALLY

ID NUMBER:

ISSUED BY:

DATE ISSUE :

EXPIRATION DATE:

WITNESS FULL NAME:

EMAIL:

PHONE NUMBER:

WITNESS SIGNATURE:

ADDRESS:

DOCUMENT TYPE:	DATE/TIME NOTARIZED:	DOCUMENT DATE:	FEE CHARGED:

COMMENTS:

RECORD NUMBER: **17**

NOTARY RECORD

FULL NAME:

EMAIL:

THUMB PRINT

PHONE NUMBER:

SIGNER'S SIGNATURE:

ADDRESS:

SERVICES PROVIDED:
- ☐ JURAT
- ☐ OATH
- ☐ ACKNOWLEDGEMENT
- ☐ OTHER : ....

IDENTIFICATION:
- ☐ ID CARD
- ☐ PASSPORT
- ☐ DRIVERS LICENSE
- ☐ OTHER : ....

- ☐ CREDIBLE WITNESS
- ☐ KNOWN PERSONALLY

ID NUMBER:

ISSUED BY:

DATE ISSUE :

EXPIRATION DATE:

WITNESS FULL NAME:

EMAIL:

PHONE NUMBER:

WITNESS SIGNATURE:

ADDRESS:

DOCUMENT TYPE:	DATE/TIME NOTARIZED:	DOCUMENT DATE:	FEE CHARGED:

COMMENTS:

RECORD NUMBER: **18**

NOTARY RECORD

FULL NAME:	EMAIL:	THUMB PRINT
PHONE NUMBER:	SIGNER'S SIGNATURE:	
ADDRESS:		

SERVICES PROVIDED:	IDENTIFICATION:		ID NUMBER:
☐ JURAT	☐ ID CARD	☐ CREDIBLE WITNESS	
☐ OATH	☐ PASSPORT	☐ KNOWN PERSONALLY	ISSUED BY:
☐ ACKNOWLEDGEMENT	☐ DRIVERS LICENSE		DATE ISSUE : / EXPIRATION DATE:
☐ OTHER :	☐ OTHER :		

WITNESS FULL NAME:	EMAIL:
PHONE NUMBER:	WITNESS SIGNATURE:
ADDRESS:	

DOCUMENT TYPE:	DATE/TIME NOTARIZED:	DOCUMENT DATE:	FEE CHARGED:
COMMENTS:		RECORD NUMBER:	**19**

NOTARY RECORD

FULL NAME:	EMAIL:	THUMB PRINT
PHONE NUMBER:	SIGNER'S SIGNATURE:	
ADDRESS:		

SERVICES PROVIDED:	IDENTIFICATION:		ID NUMBER:
☐ JURAT	☐ ID CARD	☐ CREDIBLE WITNESS	
☐ OATH	☐ PASSPORT	☐ KNOWN PERSONALLY	ISSUED BY:
☐ ACKNOWLEDGEMENT	☐ DRIVERS LICENSE		DATE ISSUE : / EXPIRATION DATE:
☐ OTHER :	☐ OTHER :		

WITNESS FULL NAME:	EMAIL:
PHONE NUMBER:	WITNESS SIGNATURE:
ADDRESS:	

DOCUMENT TYPE:	DATE/TIME NOTARIZED:	DOCUMENT DATE:	FEE CHARGED:
COMMENTS:		RECORD NUMBER:	**20**

NOTARY RECORD

FULL NAME:

EMAIL:

THUMB PRINT

PHONE NUMBER:

SIGNER'S SIGNATURE:

ADDRESS:

SERVICES PROVIDED:
- ☐ JURAT
- ☐ OATH
- ☐ ACKNOWLEDGEMENT
- ☐ OTHER : ....

IDENTIFICATION:
- ☐ ID CARD
- ☐ PASSPORT
- ☐ DRIVERS LICENSE
- ☐ OTHER : ....

- ☐ CREDIBLE WITNESS
- ☐ KNOWN PERSONALLY

ID NUMBER:

ISSUED BY:

DATE ISSUE :

EXPIRATION DATE:

WITNESS FULL NAME:

EMAIL:

PHONE NUMBER:

WITNESS SIGNATURE:

ADDRESS:

DOCUMENT TYPE:

DATE/TIME NOTARIZED:

DOCUMENT DATE:

FEE CHARGED:

COMMENTS:

RECORD NUMBER: **21**

NOTARY RECORD

FULL NAME:

EMAIL:

THUMB PRINT

PHONE NUMBER:

SIGNER'S SIGNATURE:

ADDRESS:

SERVICES PROVIDED:
- ☐ JURAT
- ☐ OATH
- ☐ ACKNOWLEDGEMENT
- ☐ OTHER : ....

IDENTIFICATION:
- ☐ ID CARD
- ☐ PASSPORT
- ☐ DRIVERS LICENSE
- ☐ OTHER : ....

- ☐ CREDIBLE WITNESS
- ☐ KNOWN PERSONALLY

ID NUMBER:

ISSUED BY:

DATE ISSUE :

EXPIRATION DATE:

WITNESS FULL NAME:

EMAIL:

PHONE NUMBER:

WITNESS SIGNATURE:

ADDRESS:

DOCUMENT TYPE:

DATE/TIME NOTARIZED:

DOCUMENT DATE:

FEE CHARGED:

COMMENTS:

RECORD NUMBER: **22**

NOTARY RECORD

FULL NAME:	EMAIL:	THUMB PRINT
PHONE NUMBER:	SIGNER'S SIGNATURE:	
ADDRESS:		

SERVICES PROVIDED:	IDENTIFICATION:		ID NUMBER:
☐ JURAT	☐ ID CARD	☐ CREDIBLE WITNESS	
☐ OATH	☐ PASSPORT	☐ KNOWN PERSONALLY	ISSUED BY:
☐ ACKNOWLEDGEMENT	☐ DRIVERS LICENSE		DATE ISSUE : / EXPIRATION DATE:
☐ OTHER :	☐ OTHER :		

WITNESS FULL NAME:	EMAIL:
PHONE NUMBER:	WITNESS SIGNATURE:
ADDRESS:	

DOCUMENT TYPE:	DATE/TIME NOTARIZED:	DOCUMENT DATE:	FEE CHARGED:
COMMENTS:			RECORD NUMBER: **23**

NOTARY RECORD

FULL NAME:	EMAIL:	THUMB PRINT
PHONE NUMBER:	SIGNER'S SIGNATURE:	
ADDRESS:		

SERVICES PROVIDED:	IDENTIFICATION:		ID NUMBER:
☐ JURAT	☐ ID CARD	☐ CREDIBLE WITNESS	
☐ OATH	☐ PASSPORT	☐ KNOWN PERSONALLY	ISSUED BY:
☐ ACKNOWLEDGEMENT	☐ DRIVERS LICENSE		DATE ISSUE : / EXPIRATION DATE:
☐ OTHER :	☐ OTHER :		

WITNESS FULL NAME:	EMAIL:
PHONE NUMBER:	WITNESS SIGNATURE:
ADDRESS:	

DOCUMENT TYPE:	DATE/TIME NOTARIZED:	DOCUMENT DATE:	FEE CHARGED:
COMMENTS:			RECORD NUMBER: **24**

NOTARY RECORD

FULL NAME:	EMAIL:	THUMB PRINT
PHONE NUMBER:	SIGNER'S SIGNATURE:	
ADDRESS:		

SERVICES PROVIDED:	IDENTIFICATION:		ID NUMBER:
☐ JURAT	☐ ID CARD	☐ CREDIBLE WITNESS	
☐ OATH	☐ PASSPORT	☐ KNOWN PERSONALLY	ISSUED BY:
☐ ACKNOWLEDGEMENT	☐ DRIVERS LICENSE		DATE ISSUE : EXPIRATION DATE:
☐ OTHER :	☐ OTHER :		

WITNESS FULL NAME:	EMAIL:
PHONE NUMBER:	WITNESS SIGNATURE:
ADDRESS:	

DOCUMENT TYPE:	DATE/TIME NOTARIZED:	DOCUMENT DATE:	FEE CHARGED:
COMMENTS:		RECORD NUMBER:	**25**

NOTARY RECORD

FULL NAME:	EMAIL:	THUMB PRINT
PHONE NUMBER:	SIGNER'S SIGNATURE:	
ADDRESS:		

SERVICES PROVIDED:	IDENTIFICATION:		ID NUMBER:
☐ JURAT	☐ ID CARD	☐ CREDIBLE WITNESS	
☐ OATH	☐ PASSPORT	☐ KNOWN PERSONALLY	ISSUED BY:
☐ ACKNOWLEDGEMENT	☐ DRIVERS LICENSE		DATE ISSUE : EXPIRATION DATE:
☐ OTHER :	☐ OTHER :		

WITNESS FULL NAME:	EMAIL:
PHONE NUMBER:	WITNESS SIGNATURE:
ADDRESS:	

DOCUMENT TYPE:	DATE/TIME NOTARIZED:	DOCUMENT DATE:	FEE CHARGED:
COMMENTS:		RECORD NUMBER:	**26**

NOTARY RECORD

FULL NAME:	EMAIL:	THUMB PRINT
PHONE NUMBER:	SIGNER'S SIGNATURE:	
ADDRESS:		

SERVICES PROVIDED:	IDENTIFICATION:		ID NUMBER:	
☐ JURAT	☐ ID CARD	☐ CREDIBLE WITNESS		
☐ OATH	☐ PASSPORT	☐ KNOWN PERSONALLY	ISSUED BY:	
☐ ACKNOWLEDGEMENT	☐ DRIVERS LICENSE		DATE ISSUE :	EXPIRATION DATE:
☐ OTHER :	☐ OTHER :			

WITNESS FULL NAME:	EMAIL:
PHONE NUMBER:	WITNESS SIGNATURE:
ADDRESS:	

DOCUMENT TYPE:	DATE/TIME NOTARIZED:	DOCUMENT DATE:	FEE CHARGED:
COMMENTS:			RECORD NUMBER: **27**

NOTARY RECORD

FULL NAME:	EMAIL:	THUMB PRINT
PHONE NUMBER:	SIGNER'S SIGNATURE:	
ADDRESS:		

SERVICES PROVIDED:	IDENTIFICATION:		ID NUMBER:	
☐ JURAT	☐ ID CARD	☐ CREDIBLE WITNESS		
☐ OATH	☐ PASSPORT	☐ KNOWN PERSONALLY	ISSUED BY:	
☐ ACKNOWLEDGEMENT	☐ DRIVERS LICENSE		DATE ISSUE :	EXPIRATION DATE:
☐ OTHER :	☐ OTHER :			

WITNESS FULL NAME:	EMAIL:
PHONE NUMBER:	WITNESS SIGNATURE:
ADDRESS:	

DOCUMENT TYPE:	DATE/TIME NOTARIZED:	DOCUMENT DATE:	FEE CHARGED:
COMMENTS:			RECORD NUMBER: **28**

NOTARY RECORD

FULL NAME:

EMAIL:

THUMB PRINT

PHONE NUMBER:

SIGNER'S SIGNATURE:

ADDRESS:

SERVICES PROVIDED:
- ☐ JURAT
- ☐ OATH
- ☐ ACKNOWLEDGEMENT
- ☐ OTHER : ....

IDENTIFICATION:
- ☐ ID CARD
- ☐ PASSPORT
- ☐ DRIVERS LICENSE
- ☐ OTHER : ....

- ☐ CREDIBLE WITNESS
- ☐ KNOWN PERSONALLY

ID NUMBER:

ISSUED BY:

DATE ISSUE :

EXPIRATION DATE:

WITNESS FULL NAME:

EMAIL:

PHONE NUMBER:

WITNESS SIGNATURE:

ADDRESS:

DOCUMENT TYPE:	DATE/TIME NOTARIZED:	DOCUMENT DATE:	FEE CHARGED:

COMMENTS:

RECORD NUMBER: **29**

NOTARY RECORD

FULL NAME:

EMAIL:

THUMB PRINT

PHONE NUMBER:

SIGNER'S SIGNATURE:

ADDRESS:

SERVICES PROVIDED:
- ☐ JURAT
- ☐ OATH
- ☐ ACKNOWLEDGEMENT
- ☐ OTHER : ....

IDENTIFICATION:
- ☐ ID CARD
- ☐ PASSPORT
- ☐ DRIVERS LICENSE
- ☐ OTHER : ....

- ☐ CREDIBLE WITNESS
- ☐ KNOWN PERSONALLY

ID NUMBER:

ISSUED BY:

DATE ISSUE :

EXPIRATION DATE:

WITNESS FULL NAME:

EMAIL:

PHONE NUMBER:

WITNESS SIGNATURE:

ADDRESS:

DOCUMENT TYPE:	DATE/TIME NOTARIZED:	DOCUMENT DATE:	FEE CHARGED:

COMMENTS:

RECORD NUMBER: **30**

NOTARY RECORD

FULL NAME:	EMAIL:	THUMB PRINT
PHONE NUMBER:	SIGNER'S SIGNATURE:	
ADDRESS:		

SERVICES PROVIDED:	IDENTIFICATION:		ID NUMBER:
☐ JURAT	☐ ID CARD	☐ CREDIBLE WITNESS	
☐ OATH	☐ PASSPORT	☐ KNOWN PERSONALLY	ISSUED BY:
☐ ACKNOWLEDGEMENT	☐ DRIVERS LICENSE		DATE ISSUE : / EXPIRATION DATE:
☐ OTHER :	☐ OTHER :		

WITNESS FULL NAME:	EMAIL:
PHONE NUMBER:	WITNESS SIGNATURE:
ADDRESS:	

DOCUMENT TYPE:	DATE/TIME NOTARIZED:	DOCUMENT DATE:	FEE CHARGED:

COMMENTS:	RECORD NUMBER: 31

NOTARY RECORD

FULL NAME:	EMAIL:	THUMB PRINT
PHONE NUMBER:	SIGNER'S SIGNATURE:	
ADDRESS:		

SERVICES PROVIDED:	IDENTIFICATION:		ID NUMBER:
☐ JURAT	☐ ID CARD	☐ CREDIBLE WITNESS	
☐ OATH	☐ PASSPORT	☐ KNOWN PERSONALLY	ISSUED BY:
☐ ACKNOWLEDGEMENT	☐ DRIVERS LICENSE		DATE ISSUE : / EXPIRATION DATE:
☐ OTHER :	☐ OTHER :		

WITNESS FULL NAME:	EMAIL:
PHONE NUMBER:	WITNESS SIGNATURE:
ADDRESS:	

DOCUMENT TYPE:	DATE/TIME NOTARIZED:	DOCUMENT DATE:	FEE CHARGED:

COMMENTS:	RECORD NUMBER: 32

NOTARY RECORD

FULL NAME:

EMAIL:

THUMB PRINT

PHONE NUMBER:

SIGNER'S SIGNATURE:

ADDRESS:

SERVICES PROVIDED:
- ☐ JURAT
- ☐ OATH
- ☐ ACKNOWLEDGEMENT
- ☐ OTHER : ....

IDENTIFICATION:
- ☐ ID CARD
- ☐ PASSPORT
- ☐ DRIVERS LICENSE
- ☐ OTHER : ....
- ☐ CREDIBLE WITNESS
- ☐ KNOWN PERSONALLY

ID NUMBER:

ISSUED BY:

DATE ISSUE :

EXPIRATION DATE:

WITNESS FULL NAME:

EMAIL:

PHONE NUMBER:

WITNESS SIGNATURE:

ADDRESS:

DOCUMENT TYPE:

DATE/TIME NOTARIZED:

DOCUMENT DATE:

FEE CHARGED:

COMMENTS:

RECORD NUMBER: **33**

NOTARY RECORD

FULL NAME:

EMAIL:

THUMB PRINT

PHONE NUMBER:

SIGNER'S SIGNATURE:

ADDRESS:

SERVICES PROVIDED:
- ☐ JURAT
- ☐ OATH
- ☐ ACKNOWLEDGEMENT
- ☐ OTHER : ....

IDENTIFICATION:
- ☐ ID CARD
- ☐ PASSPORT
- ☐ DRIVERS LICENSE
- ☐ OTHER : ....
- ☐ CREDIBLE WITNESS
- ☐ KNOWN PERSONALLY

ID NUMBER:

ISSUED BY:

DATE ISSUE :

EXPIRATION DATE:

WITNESS FULL NAME:

EMAIL:

PHONE NUMBER:

WITNESS SIGNATURE:

ADDRESS:

DOCUMENT TYPE:

DATE/TIME NOTARIZED:

DOCUMENT DATE:

FEE CHARGED:

COMMENTS:

RECORD NUMBER: **34**

NOTARY RECORD

FULL NAME:	EMAIL:	THUMB PRINT
PHONE NUMBER:	SIGNER'S SIGNATURE:	
ADDRESS:		

SERVICES PROVIDED:	IDENTIFICATION:		ID NUMBER:
☐ JURAT	☐ ID CARD	☐ CREDIBLE WITNESS	
☐ OATH	☐ PASSPORT	☐ KNOWN PERSONALLY	ISSUED BY:
☐ ACKNOWLEDGEMENT	☐ DRIVERS LICENSE		DATE ISSUE : / EXPIRATION DATE:
☐ OTHER :	☐ OTHER :		

WITNESS FULL NAME:	EMAIL:
PHONE NUMBER:	WITNESS SIGNATURE:
ADDRESS:	

DOCUMENT TYPE:	DATE/TIME NOTARIZED:	DOCUMENT DATE:	FEE CHARGED:
COMMENTS:			RECORD NUMBER: **35**

NOTARY RECORD

FULL NAME:	EMAIL:	THUMB PRINT
PHONE NUMBER:	SIGNER'S SIGNATURE:	
ADDRESS:		

SERVICES PROVIDED:	IDENTIFICATION:		ID NUMBER:
☐ JURAT	☐ ID CARD	☐ CREDIBLE WITNESS	
☐ OATH	☐ PASSPORT	☐ KNOWN PERSONALLY	ISSUED BY:
☐ ACKNOWLEDGEMENT	☐ DRIVERS LICENSE		DATE ISSUE : / EXPIRATION DATE:
☐ OTHER :	☐ OTHER :		

WITNESS FULL NAME:	EMAIL:
PHONE NUMBER:	WITNESS SIGNATURE:
ADDRESS:	

DOCUMENT TYPE:	DATE/TIME NOTARIZED:	DOCUMENT DATE:	FEE CHARGED:
COMMENTS:			RECORD NUMBER: **36**

NOTARY RECORD

FULL NAME:	EMAIL:	THUMB PRINT
PHONE NUMBER:	SIGNER'S SIGNATURE:	
ADDRESS:		

SERVICES PROVIDED:	IDENTIFICATION:		ID NUMBER:
☐ JURAT	☐ ID CARD	☐ CREDIBLE WITNESS	
☐ OATH	☐ PASSPORT	☐ KNOWN PERSONALLY	ISSUED BY:
☐ ACKNOWLEDGEMENT	☐ DRIVERS LICENSE		DATE ISSUE : / EXPIRATION DATE:
☐ OTHER :	☐ OTHER :		

WITNESS FULL NAME:	EMAIL:
PHONE NUMBER:	WITNESS SIGNATURE:
ADDRESS:	

DOCUMENT TYPE:	DATE/TIME NOTARIZED:	DOCUMENT DATE:	FEE CHARGED:
COMMENTS:			RECORD NUMBER: 37

NOTARY RECORD

FULL NAME:	EMAIL:	THUMB PRINT
PHONE NUMBER:	SIGNER'S SIGNATURE:	
ADDRESS:		

SERVICES PROVIDED:	IDENTIFICATION:		ID NUMBER:
☐ JURAT	☐ ID CARD	☐ CREDIBLE WITNESS	
☐ OATH	☐ PASSPORT	☐ KNOWN PERSONALLY	ISSUED BY:
☐ ACKNOWLEDGEMENT	☐ DRIVERS LICENSE		DATE ISSUE : / EXPIRATION DATE:
☐ OTHER :	☐ OTHER :		

WITNESS FULL NAME:	EMAIL:
PHONE NUMBER:	WITNESS SIGNATURE:
ADDRESS:	

DOCUMENT TYPE:	DATE/TIME NOTARIZED:	DOCUMENT DATE:	FEE CHARGED:
COMMENTS:			RECORD NUMBER: 38

NOTARY RECORD

FULL NAME:	EMAIL:	THUMB PRINT
PHONE NUMBER:	SIGNER'S SIGNATURE:	
ADDRESS:		

SERVICES PROVIDED:	IDENTIFICATION:		ID NUMBER:
☐ JURAT	☐ ID CARD	☐ CREDIBLE WITNESS	
☐ OATH	☐ PASSPORT	☐ KNOWN PERSONALLY	ISSUED BY:
☐ ACKNOWLEDGEMENT	☐ DRIVERS LICENSE		DATE ISSUE : / EXPIRATION DATE:
☐ OTHER :	☐ OTHER :		

WITNESS FULL NAME:	EMAIL:
PHONE NUMBER:	WITNESS SIGNATURE:
ADDRESS:	

DOCUMENT TYPE:	DATE/TIME NOTARIZED:	DOCUMENT DATE:	FEE CHARGED:
COMMENTS:			RECORD NUMBER: **39**

NOTARY RECORD

FULL NAME:	EMAIL:	THUMB PRINT
PHONE NUMBER:	SIGNER'S SIGNATURE:	
ADDRESS:		

SERVICES PROVIDED:	IDENTIFICATION:		ID NUMBER:
☐ JURAT	☐ ID CARD	☐ CREDIBLE WITNESS	
☐ OATH	☐ PASSPORT	☐ KNOWN PERSONALLY	ISSUED BY:
☐ ACKNOWLEDGEMENT	☐ DRIVERS LICENSE		DATE ISSUE : / EXPIRATION DATE:
☐ OTHER :	☐ OTHER :		

WITNESS FULL NAME:	EMAIL:
PHONE NUMBER:	WITNESS SIGNATURE:
ADDRESS:	

DOCUMENT TYPE:	DATE/TIME NOTARIZED:	DOCUMENT DATE:	FEE CHARGED:
COMMENTS:			RECORD NUMBER: **40**

NOTARY RECORD

FULL NAME:

EMAIL:

THUMB PRINT

PHONE NUMBER:

SIGNER'S SIGNATURE:

ADDRESS:

SERVICES PROVIDED:	IDENTIFICATION:		ID NUMBER:
☐ JURAT	☐ ID CARD	☐ CREDIBLE WITNESS	
☐ OATH	☐ PASSPORT	☐ KNOWN PERSONALLY	ISSUED BY:
☐ ACKNOWLEDGEMENT	☐ DRIVERS LICENSE		DATE ISSUE :
☐ OTHER :	☐ OTHER :		EXPIRATION DATE:

WITNESS FULL NAME:

EMAIL:

PHONE NUMBER:

WITNESS SIGNATURE:

ADDRESS:

DOCUMENT TYPE:	DATE/TIME NOTARIZED:	DOCUMENT DATE:	FEE CHARGED:

COMMENTS:

RECORD NUMBER: **41**

NOTARY RECORD

FULL NAME:

EMAIL:

THUMB PRINT

PHONE NUMBER:

SIGNER'S SIGNATURE:

ADDRESS:

SERVICES PROVIDED:	IDENTIFICATION:		ID NUMBER:
☐ JURAT	☐ ID CARD	☐ CREDIBLE WITNESS	
☐ OATH	☐ PASSPORT	☐ KNOWN PERSONALLY	ISSUED BY:
☐ ACKNOWLEDGEMENT	☐ DRIVERS LICENSE		DATE ISSUE :
☐ OTHER :	☐ OTHER :		EXPIRATION DATE:

WITNESS FULL NAME:

EMAIL:

PHONE NUMBER:

WITNESS SIGNATURE:

ADDRESS:

DOCUMENT TYPE:	DATE/TIME NOTARIZED:	DOCUMENT DATE:	FEE CHARGED:

COMMENTS:

RECORD NUMBER: **42**

NOTARY RECORD

FULL NAME:	EMAIL:	THUMB PRINT
PHONE NUMBER:	SIGNER'S SIGNATURE:	
ADDRESS:		

SERVICES PROVIDED:	IDENTIFICATION:		ID NUMBER:
☐ JURAT	☐ ID CARD	☐ CREDIBLE WITNESS	
☐ OATH	☐ PASSPORT	☐ KNOWN PERSONALLY	ISSUED BY:
☐ ACKNOWLEDGEMENT	☐ DRIVERS LICENSE		DATE ISSUE : / EXPIRATION DATE:
☐ OTHER :	☐ OTHER :		

WITNESS FULL NAME:	EMAIL:
PHONE NUMBER:	WITNESS SIGNATURE:
ADDRESS:	

DOCUMENT TYPE:	DATE/TIME NOTARIZED:	DOCUMENT DATE:	FEE CHARGED:
COMMENTS:			RECORD NUMBER: **43**

NOTARY RECORD

FULL NAME:	EMAIL:	THUMB PRINT
PHONE NUMBER:	SIGNER'S SIGNATURE:	
ADDRESS:		

SERVICES PROVIDED:	IDENTIFICATION:		ID NUMBER:
☐ JURAT	☐ ID CARD	☐ CREDIBLE WITNESS	
☐ OATH	☐ PASSPORT	☐ KNOWN PERSONALLY	ISSUED BY:
☐ ACKNOWLEDGEMENT	☐ DRIVERS LICENSE		DATE ISSUE : / EXPIRATION DATE:
☐ OTHER :	☐ OTHER :		

WITNESS FULL NAME:	EMAIL:
PHONE NUMBER:	WITNESS SIGNATURE:
ADDRESS:	

DOCUMENT TYPE:	DATE/TIME NOTARIZED:	DOCUMENT DATE:	FEE CHARGED:
COMMENTS:			RECORD NUMBER: **44**

NOTARY RECORD

FULL NAME:

EMAIL:

THUMB PRINT

PHONE NUMBER:

SIGNER'S SIGNATURE:

ADDRESS:

SERVICES PROVIDED:	IDENTIFICATION:		ID NUMBER:
☐ JURAT	☐ ID CARD	☐ CREDIBLE WITNESS	
☐ OATH	☐ PASSPORT	☐ KNOWN PERSONALLY	ISSUED BY:
☐ ACKNOWLEDGEMENT	☐ DRIVERS LICENSE		DATE ISSUE : / EXPIRATION DATE:
☐ OTHER :	☐ OTHER :		

WITNESS FULL NAME:

EMAIL:

PHONE NUMBER:

WITNESS SIGNATURE:

ADDRESS:

DOCUMENT TYPE:	DATE/TIME NOTARIZED:	DOCUMENT DATE:	FEE CHARGED:

COMMENTS:

RECORD NUMBER: **45**

NOTARY RECORD

FULL NAME:

EMAIL:

THUMB PRINT

PHONE NUMBER:

SIGNER'S SIGNATURE:

ADDRESS:

SERVICES PROVIDED:	IDENTIFICATION:		ID NUMBER:
☐ JURAT	☐ ID CARD	☐ CREDIBLE WITNESS	
☐ OATH	☐ PASSPORT	☐ KNOWN PERSONALLY	ISSUED BY:
☐ ACKNOWLEDGEMENT	☐ DRIVERS LICENSE		DATE ISSUE : / EXPIRATION DATE:
☐ OTHER :	☐ OTHER :		

WITNESS FULL NAME:

EMAIL:

PHONE NUMBER:

WITNESS SIGNATURE:

ADDRESS:

DOCUMENT TYPE:	DATE/TIME NOTARIZED:	DOCUMENT DATE:	FEE CHARGED:

COMMENTS:

RECORD NUMBER: **46**

NOTARY RECORD

FULL NAME:	EMAIL:	THUMB PRINT
PHONE NUMBER:	SIGNER'S SIGNATURE:	
ADDRESS:		

SERVICES PROVIDED:	IDENTIFICATION:		ID NUMBER:
☐ JURAT	☐ ID CARD	☐ CREDIBLE WITNESS	
☐ OATH	☐ PASSPORT	☐ KNOWN PERSONALLY	ISSUED BY:
☐ ACKNOWLEDGEMENT	☐ DRIVERS LICENSE		DATE ISSUE : / EXPIRATION DATE:
☐ OTHER :	☐ OTHER :		

WITNESS FULL NAME:	EMAIL:
PHONE NUMBER:	WITNESS SIGNATURE:
ADDRESS:	

DOCUMENT TYPE:	DATE/TIME NOTARIZED:	DOCUMENT DATE:	FEE CHARGED:

COMMENTS:	RECORD NUMBER: 47

NOTARY RECORD

FULL NAME:	EMAIL:	THUMB PRINT
PHONE NUMBER:	SIGNER'S SIGNATURE:	
ADDRESS:		

SERVICES PROVIDED:	IDENTIFICATION:		ID NUMBER:
☐ JURAT	☐ ID CARD	☐ CREDIBLE WITNESS	
☐ OATH	☐ PASSPORT	☐ KNOWN PERSONALLY	ISSUED BY:
☐ ACKNOWLEDGEMENT	☐ DRIVERS LICENSE		DATE ISSUE : / EXPIRATION DATE:
☐ OTHER :	☐ OTHER :		

WITNESS FULL NAME:	EMAIL:
PHONE NUMBER:	WITNESS SIGNATURE:
ADDRESS:	

DOCUMENT TYPE:	DATE/TIME NOTARIZED:	DOCUMENT DATE:	FEE CHARGED:

COMMENTS:	RECORD NUMBER: 48

NOTARY RECORD

FULL NAME:

EMAIL:

THUMB PRINT

PHONE NUMBER:

SIGNER'S SIGNATURE:

ADDRESS:

SERVICES PROVIDED:	IDENTIFICATION:		ID NUMBER:
☐ JURAT	☐ ID CARD	☐ CREDIBLE WITNESS	
☐ OATH	☐ PASSPORT	☐ KNOWN PERSONALLY	ISSUED BY:
☐ ACKNOWLEDGEMENT	☐ DRIVERS LICENSE		DATE ISSUE : / EXPIRATION DATE:
☐ OTHER :	☐ OTHER :		

WITNESS FULL NAME:

EMAIL:

PHONE NUMBER:

WITNESS SIGNATURE:

ADDRESS:

DOCUMENT TYPE:	DATE/TIME NOTARIZED:	DOCUMENT DATE:	FEE CHARGED:

COMMENTS:

RECORD NUMBER: **459**

NOTARY RECORD

FULL NAME:

EMAIL:

THUMB PRINT

PHONE NUMBER:

SIGNER'S SIGNATURE:

ADDRESS:

SERVICES PROVIDED:	IDENTIFICATION:		ID NUMBER:
☐ JURAT	☐ ID CARD	☐ CREDIBLE WITNESS	
☐ OATH	☐ PASSPORT	☐ KNOWN PERSONALLY	ISSUED BY:
☐ ACKNOWLEDGEMENT	☐ DRIVERS LICENSE		DATE ISSUE : / EXPIRATION DATE:
☐ OTHER :	☐ OTHER :		

WITNESS FULL NAME:

EMAIL:

PHONE NUMBER:

WITNESS SIGNATURE:

ADDRESS:

DOCUMENT TYPE:	DATE/TIME NOTARIZED:	DOCUMENT DATE:	FEE CHARGED:

COMMENTS:

RECORD NUMBER: **50**

NOTARY RECORD

FULL NAME:	EMAIL:	THUMB PRINT
PHONE NUMBER:	SIGNER'S SIGNATURE:	
ADDRESS:		

SERVICES PROVIDED:	IDENTIFICATION:		ID NUMBER:	
☐ JURAT	☐ ID CARD	☐ CREDIBLE WITNESS		
☐ OATH	☐ PASSPORT	☐ KNOWN PERSONALLY	ISSUED BY:	
☐ ACKNOWLEDGEMENT	☐ DRIVERS LICENSE		DATE ISSUE :	EXPIRATION DATE:
☐ OTHER :	☐ OTHER :			

WITNESS FULL NAME:	EMAIL:
PHONE NUMBER:	WITNESS SIGNATURE:
ADDRESS:	

DOCUMENT TYPE:	DATE/TIME NOTARIZED:	DOCUMENT DATE:	FEE CHARGED:

COMMENTS:	RECORD NUMBER: 51

NOTARY RECORD

FULL NAME:	EMAIL:	THUMB PRINT
PHONE NUMBER:	SIGNER'S SIGNATURE:	
ADDRESS:		

SERVICES PROVIDED:	IDENTIFICATION:		ID NUMBER:	
☐ JURAT	☐ ID CARD	☐ CREDIBLE WITNESS		
☐ OATH	☐ PASSPORT	☐ KNOWN PERSONALLY	ISSUED BY:	
☐ ACKNOWLEDGEMENT	☐ DRIVERS LICENSE		DATE ISSUE :	EXPIRATION DATE:
☐ OTHER :	☐ OTHER :			

WITNESS FULL NAME:	EMAIL:
PHONE NUMBER:	WITNESS SIGNATURE:
ADDRESS:	

DOCUMENT TYPE:	DATE/TIME NOTARIZED:	DOCUMENT DATE:	FEE CHARGED:

COMMENTS:	RECORD NUMBER: 52

NOTARY RECORD

FULL NAME:	EMAIL:	THUMB PRINT
PHONE NUMBER:	SIGNER'S SIGNATURE:	
ADDRESS:		

SERVICES PROVIDED:	IDENTIFICATION:		ID NUMBER:
☐ JURAT	☐ ID CARD	☐ CREDIBLE WITNESS	
☐ OATH	☐ PASSPORT	☐ KNOWN PERSONALLY	ISSUED BY:
☐ ACKNOWLEDGEMENT	☐ DRIVERS LICENSE		DATE ISSUE : / EXPIRATION DATE:
☐ OTHER :	☐ OTHER :		

WITNESS FULL NAME:	EMAIL:
PHONE NUMBER:	WITNESS SIGNATURE:
ADDRESS:	

DOCUMENT TYPE:	DATE/TIME NOTARIZED:	DOCUMENT DATE:	FEE CHARGED:

COMMENTS:	RECORD NUMBER: 53

NOTARY RECORD

FULL NAME:	EMAIL:	THUMB PRINT
PHONE NUMBER:	SIGNER'S SIGNATURE:	
ADDRESS:		

SERVICES PROVIDED:	IDENTIFICATION:		ID NUMBER:
☐ JURAT	☐ ID CARD	☐ CREDIBLE WITNESS	
☐ OATH	☐ PASSPORT	☐ KNOWN PERSONALLY	ISSUED BY:
☐ ACKNOWLEDGEMENT	☐ DRIVERS LICENSE		DATE ISSUE : / EXPIRATION DATE:
☐ OTHER :	☐ OTHER :		

WITNESS FULL NAME:	EMAIL:
PHONE NUMBER:	WITNESS SIGNATURE:
ADDRESS:	

DOCUMENT TYPE:	DATE/TIME NOTARIZED:	DOCUMENT DATE:	FEE CHARGED:

COMMENTS:	RECORD NUMBER: 54

NOTARY RECORD

FULL NAME:	EMAIL:	THUMB PRINT
PHONE NUMBER:	SIGNER'S SIGNATURE:	
ADDRESS:		

SERVICES PROVIDED:	IDENTIFICATION:		ID NUMBER:
☐ JURAT	☐ ID CARD	☐ CREDIBLE WITNESS	
☐ OATH	☐ PASSPORT	☐ KNOWN PERSONALLY	ISSUED BY:
☐ ACKNOWLEDGEMENT	☐ DRIVERS LICENSE		DATE ISSUE : / EXPIRATION DATE:
☐ OTHER :	☐ OTHER :		

WITNESS FULL NAME:	EMAIL:
PHONE NUMBER:	WITNESS SIGNATURE:
ADDRESS:	

DOCUMENT TYPE:	DATE/TIME NOTARIZED:	DOCUMENT DATE:	FEE CHARGED:
COMMENTS:			RECORD NUMBER: **55**

NOTARY RECORD

FULL NAME:	EMAIL:	THUMB PRINT
PHONE NUMBER:	SIGNER'S SIGNATURE:	
ADDRESS:		

SERVICES PROVIDED:	IDENTIFICATION:		ID NUMBER:
☐ JURAT	☐ ID CARD	☐ CREDIBLE WITNESS	
☐ OATH	☐ PASSPORT	☐ KNOWN PERSONALLY	ISSUED BY:
☐ ACKNOWLEDGEMENT	☐ DRIVERS LICENSE		DATE ISSUE : / EXPIRATION DATE:
☐ OTHER :	☐ OTHER :		

WITNESS FULL NAME:	EMAIL:
PHONE NUMBER:	WITNESS SIGNATURE:
ADDRESS:	

DOCUMENT TYPE:	DATE/TIME NOTARIZED:	DOCUMENT DATE:	FEE CHARGED:
COMMENTS:			RECORD NUMBER: **56**

NOTARY RECORD

FULL NAME:

EMAIL:

THUMB PRINT

PHONE NUMBER:

SIGNER'S SIGNATURE:

ADDRESS:

SERVICES PROVIDED:	IDENTIFICATION:		
☐ JURAT	☐ ID CARD	☐ CREDIBLE WITNESS	**ID NUMBER:**
☐ OATH	☐ PASSPORT	☐ KNOWN PERSONALLY	**ISSUED BY:**
☐ ACKNOWLEDGEMENT	☐ DRIVERS LICENSE		**DATE ISSUE :** / **EXPIRATION DATE:**
☐ OTHER :	☐ OTHER :		

WITNESS FULL NAME:

EMAIL:

PHONE NUMBER:

WITNESS SIGNATURE:

ADDRESS:

DOCUMENT TYPE:	DATE/TIME NOTARIZED:	DOCUMENT DATE:	FEE CHARGED:

COMMENTS:	RECORD NUMBER: **57**

NOTARY RECORD

FULL NAME:

EMAIL:

THUMB PRINT

PHONE NUMBER:

SIGNER'S SIGNATURE:

ADDRESS:

SERVICES PROVIDED:	IDENTIFICATION:		
☐ JURAT	☐ ID CARD	☐ CREDIBLE WITNESS	**ID NUMBER:**
☐ OATH	☐ PASSPORT	☐ KNOWN PERSONALLY	**ISSUED BY:**
☐ ACKNOWLEDGEMENT	☐ DRIVERS LICENSE		**DATE ISSUE :** / **EXPIRATION DATE:**
☐ OTHER :	☐ OTHER :		

WITNESS FULL NAME:

EMAIL:

PHONE NUMBER:

WITNESS SIGNATURE:

ADDRESS:

DOCUMENT TYPE:	DATE/TIME NOTARIZED:	DOCUMENT DATE:	FEE CHARGED:

COMMENTS:	RECORD NUMBER: **58**

NOTARY RECORD

FULL NAME:	EMAIL:	THUMB PRINT
PHONE NUMBER:	SIGNER'S SIGNATURE:	
ADDRESS:		

SERVICES PROVIDED:	IDENTIFICATION:		ID NUMBER:
☐ JURAT	☐ ID CARD	☐ CREDIBLE WITNESS	
☐ OATH	☐ PASSPORT	☐ KNOWN PERSONALLY	ISSUED BY:
☐ ACKNOWLEDGEMENT	☐ DRIVERS LICENSE		DATE ISSUE :
☐ OTHER :	☐ OTHER :		EXPIRATION DATE:

WITNESS FULL NAME:	EMAIL:
PHONE NUMBER:	WITNESS SIGNATURE:
ADDRESS:	

DOCUMENT TYPE:	DATE/TIME NOTARIZED:	DOCUMENT DATE:	FEE CHARGED:

COMMENTS:	RECORD NUMBER: 59

NOTARY RECORD

FULL NAME:	EMAIL:	THUMB PRINT
PHONE NUMBER:	SIGNER'S SIGNATURE:	
ADDRESS:		

SERVICES PROVIDED:	IDENTIFICATION:		ID NUMBER:
☐ JURAT	☐ ID CARD	☐ CREDIBLE WITNESS	
☐ OATH	☐ PASSPORT	☐ KNOWN PERSONALLY	ISSUED BY:
☐ ACKNOWLEDGEMENT	☐ DRIVERS LICENSE		DATE ISSUE :
☐ OTHER :	☐ OTHER :		EXPIRATION DATE:

WITNESS FULL NAME:	EMAIL:
PHONE NUMBER:	WITNESS SIGNATURE:
ADDRESS:	

DOCUMENT TYPE:	DATE/TIME NOTARIZED:	DOCUMENT DATE:	FEE CHARGED:

COMMENTS:	RECORD NUMBER: 60

NOTARY RECORD

FULL NAME:	EMAIL:	THUMB PRINT
PHONE NUMBER:	SIGNER'S SIGNATURE:	
ADDRESS:		

SERVICES PROVIDED:	IDENTIFICATION:		ID NUMBER:
☐ JURAT	☐ ID CARD	☐ CREDIBLE WITNESS	
☐ OATH	☐ PASSPORT	☐ KNOWN PERSONALLY	ISSUED BY:
☐ ACKNOWLEDGEMENT	☐ DRIVERS LICENSE		DATE ISSUE : / EXPIRATION DATE:
☐ OTHER :	☐ OTHER :		

WITNESS FULL NAME:	EMAIL:
PHONE NUMBER:	WITNESS SIGNATURE:
ADDRESS:	

DOCUMENT TYPE:	DATE/TIME NOTARIZED:	DOCUMENT DATE:	FEE CHARGED:
COMMENTS:			RECORD NUMBER: **61**

NOTARY RECORD

FULL NAME:	EMAIL:	THUMB PRINT
PHONE NUMBER:	SIGNER'S SIGNATURE:	
ADDRESS:		

SERVICES PROVIDED:	IDENTIFICATION:		ID NUMBER:
☐ JURAT	☐ ID CARD	☐ CREDIBLE WITNESS	
☐ OATH	☐ PASSPORT	☐ KNOWN PERSONALLY	ISSUED BY:
☐ ACKNOWLEDGEMENT	☐ DRIVERS LICENSE		DATE ISSUE : / EXPIRATION DATE:
☐ OTHER :	☐ OTHER :		

WITNESS FULL NAME:	EMAIL:
PHONE NUMBER:	WITNESS SIGNATURE:
ADDRESS:	

DOCUMENT TYPE:	DATE/TIME NOTARIZED:	DOCUMENT DATE:	FEE CHARGED:
COMMENTS:			RECORD NUMBER: **62**

NOTARY RECORD

FULL NAME:	EMAIL:	THUMB PRINT
PHONE NUMBER:	SIGNER'S SIGNATURE:	
ADDRESS:		

SERVICES PROVIDED:	IDENTIFICATION:		ID NUMBER:
☐ JURAT	☐ ID CARD	☐ CREDIBLE WITNESS	
☐ OATH	☐ PASSPORT	☐ KNOWN PERSONALLY	ISSUED BY:
☐ ACKNOWLEDGEMENT	☐ DRIVERS LICENSE		DATE ISSUE : / EXPIRATION DATE:
☐ OTHER :	☐ OTHER :		

WITNESS FULL NAME:	EMAIL:
PHONE NUMBER:	WITNESS SIGNATURE:
ADDRESS:	

DOCUMENT TYPE:	DATE/TIME NOTARIZED:	DOCUMENT DATE:	FEE CHARGED:

COMMENTS:	RECORD NUMBER: 63

NOTARY RECORD

FULL NAME:	EMAIL:	THUMB PRINT
PHONE NUMBER:	SIGNER'S SIGNATURE:	
ADDRESS:		

SERVICES PROVIDED:	IDENTIFICATION:		ID NUMBER:
☐ JURAT	☐ ID CARD	☐ CREDIBLE WITNESS	
☐ OATH	☐ PASSPORT	☐ KNOWN PERSONALLY	ISSUED BY:
☐ ACKNOWLEDGEMENT	☐ DRIVERS LICENSE		DATE ISSUE : / EXPIRATION DATE:
☐ OTHER :	☐ OTHER :		

WITNESS FULL NAME:	EMAIL:
PHONE NUMBER:	WITNESS SIGNATURE:
ADDRESS:	

DOCUMENT TYPE:	DATE/TIME NOTARIZED:	DOCUMENT DATE:	FEE CHARGED:

COMMENTS:	RECORD NUMBER: 64

NOTARY RECORD

FULL NAME:

EMAIL:

THUMB PRINT

PHONE NUMBER:

SIGNER'S SIGNATURE:

ADDRESS:

SERVICES PROVIDED:	IDENTIFICATION:		ID NUMBER:
☐ JURAT	☐ ID CARD	☐ CREDIBLE WITNESS	
☐ OATH	☐ PASSPORT	☐ KNOWN PERSONALLY	ISSUED BY:
☐ ACKNOWLEDGEMENT	☐ DRIVERS LICENSE		DATE ISSUE : / EXPIRATION DATE:
☐ OTHER :	☐ OTHER :		

WITNESS FULL NAME:

EMAIL:

PHONE NUMBER:

WITNESS SIGNATURE:

ADDRESS:

DOCUMENT TYPE:	DATE/TIME NOTARIZED:	DOCUMENT DATE:	FEE CHARGED:

COMMENTS:	RECORD NUMBER: **65**

NOTARY RECORD

FULL NAME:

EMAIL:

THUMB PRINT

PHONE NUMBER:

SIGNER'S SIGNATURE:

ADDRESS:

SERVICES PROVIDED:	IDENTIFICATION:		ID NUMBER:
☐ JURAT	☐ ID CARD	☐ CREDIBLE WITNESS	
☐ OATH	☐ PASSPORT	☐ KNOWN PERSONALLY	ISSUED BY:
☐ ACKNOWLEDGEMENT	☐ DRIVERS LICENSE		DATE ISSUE : / EXPIRATION DATE:
☐ OTHER :	☐ OTHER :		

WITNESS FULL NAME:

EMAIL:

PHONE NUMBER:

WITNESS SIGNATURE:

ADDRESS:

DOCUMENT TYPE:	DATE/TIME NOTARIZED:	DOCUMENT DATE:	FEE CHARGED:

COMMENTS:	RECORD NUMBER: **66**

NOTARY RECORD

FULL NAME:	EMAIL:	THUMB PRINT
PHONE NUMBER:	SIGNER'S SIGNATURE:	
ADDRESS:		

SERVICES PROVIDED:	IDENTIFICATION:		ID NUMBER:
☐ JURAT	☐ ID CARD	☐ CREDIBLE WITNESS	
☐ OATH	☐ PASSPORT	☐ KNOWN PERSONALLY	ISSUED BY:
☐ ACKNOWLEDGEMENT	☐ DRIVERS LICENSE		DATE ISSUE : / EXPIRATION DATE:
☐ OTHER :	☐ OTHER :		

WITNESS FULL NAME:	EMAIL:
PHONE NUMBER:	WITNESS SIGNATURE:
ADDRESS:	

DOCUMENT TYPE:	DATE/TIME NOTARIZED:	DOCUMENT DATE:	FEE CHARGED:
COMMENTS:		RECORD NUMBER:	**67**

NOTARY RECORD

FULL NAME:	EMAIL:	THUMB PRINT
PHONE NUMBER:	SIGNER'S SIGNATURE:	
ADDRESS:		

SERVICES PROVIDED:	IDENTIFICATION:		ID NUMBER:
☐ JURAT	☐ ID CARD	☐ CREDIBLE WITNESS	
☐ OATH	☐ PASSPORT	☐ KNOWN PERSONALLY	ISSUED BY:
☐ ACKNOWLEDGEMENT	☐ DRIVERS LICENSE		DATE ISSUE : / EXPIRATION DATE:
☐ OTHER :	☐ OTHER :		

WITNESS FULL NAME:	EMAIL:
PHONE NUMBER:	WITNESS SIGNATURE:
ADDRESS:	

DOCUMENT TYPE:	DATE/TIME NOTARIZED:	DOCUMENT DATE:	FEE CHARGED:
COMMENTS:		RECORD NUMBER:	**68**

NOTARY RECORD

FULL NAME:	EMAIL:	THUMB PRINT
PHONE NUMBER:	SIGNER'S SIGNATURE:	
ADDRESS:		

SERVICES PROVIDED:	IDENTIFICATION:		ID NUMBER:
☐ JURAT	☐ ID CARD	☐ CREDIBLE WITNESS	
☐ OATH	☐ PASSPORT	☐ KNOWN PERSONALLY	ISSUED BY:
☐ ACKNOWLEDGEMENT	☐ DRIVERS LICENSE		DATE ISSUE : / EXPIRATION DATE:
☐ OTHER :	☐ OTHER :		

WITNESS FULL NAME:	EMAIL:
PHONE NUMBER:	WITNESS SIGNATURE:
ADDRESS:	

DOCUMENT TYPE:	DATE/TIME NOTARIZED:	DOCUMENT DATE:	FEE CHARGED:

COMMENTS:	RECORD NUMBER: 69

NOTARY RECORD

FULL NAME:	EMAIL:	THUMB PRINT
PHONE NUMBER:	SIGNER'S SIGNATURE:	
ADDRESS:		

SERVICES PROVIDED:	IDENTIFICATION:		ID NUMBER:
☐ JURAT	☐ ID CARD	☐ CREDIBLE WITNESS	
☐ OATH	☐ PASSPORT	☐ KNOWN PERSONALLY	ISSUED BY:
☐ ACKNOWLEDGEMENT	☐ DRIVERS LICENSE		DATE ISSUE : / EXPIRATION DATE:
☐ OTHER :	☐ OTHER :		

WITNESS FULL NAME:	EMAIL:
PHONE NUMBER:	WITNESS SIGNATURE:
ADDRESS:	

DOCUMENT TYPE:	DATE/TIME NOTARIZED:	DOCUMENT DATE:	FEE CHARGED:

COMMENTS:	RECORD NUMBER: 70

NOTARY RECORD

FULL NAME:	EMAIL:	THUMB PRINT
PHONE NUMBER:	SIGNER'S SIGNATURE:	
ADDRESS:		

SERVICES PROVIDED:	IDENTIFICATION:		ID NUMBER:
☐ JURAT	☐ ID CARD	☐ CREDIBLE WITNESS	
☐ OATH	☐ PASSPORT	☐ KNOWN PERSONALLY	ISSUED BY:
☐ ACKNOWLEDGEMENT	☐ DRIVERS LICENSE		DATE ISSUE :
☐ OTHER :	☐ OTHER :		EXPIRATION DATE:

WITNESS FULL NAME:	EMAIL:
PHONE NUMBER:	WITNESS SIGNATURE:
ADDRESS:	

DOCUMENT TYPE:	DATE/TIME NOTARIZED:	DOCUMENT DATE:	FEE CHARGED:
COMMENTS:			RECORD NUMBER: 71

NOTARY RECORD

FULL NAME:	EMAIL:	THUMB PRINT
PHONE NUMBER:	SIGNER'S SIGNATURE:	
ADDRESS:		

SERVICES PROVIDED:	IDENTIFICATION:		ID NUMBER:
☐ JURAT	☐ ID CARD	☐ CREDIBLE WITNESS	
☐ OATH	☐ PASSPORT	☐ KNOWN PERSONALLY	ISSUED BY:
☐ ACKNOWLEDGEMENT	☐ DRIVERS LICENSE		DATE ISSUE :
☐ OTHER :	☐ OTHER :		EXPIRATION DATE:

WITNESS FULL NAME:	EMAIL:
PHONE NUMBER:	WITNESS SIGNATURE:
ADDRESS:	

DOCUMENT TYPE:	DATE/TIME NOTARIZED:	DOCUMENT DATE:	FEE CHARGED:
COMMENTS:			RECORD NUMBER: 72

NOTARY RECORD

FULL NAME:	EMAIL:	THUMB PRINT
PHONE NUMBER:	SIGNER'S SIGNATURE:	
ADDRESS:		

SERVICES PROVIDED:	IDENTIFICATION:		ID NUMBER:
☐ JURAT	☐ ID CARD	☐ CREDIBLE WITNESS	
☐ OATH	☐ PASSPORT	☐ KNOWN PERSONALLY	ISSUED BY:
☐ ACKNOWLEDGEMENT	☐ DRIVERS LICENSE		DATE ISSUE : / EXPIRATION DATE:
☐ OTHER :	☐ OTHER :		

WITNESS FULL NAME:	EMAIL:
PHONE NUMBER:	WITNESS SIGNATURE:
ADDRESS:	

DOCUMENT TYPE:	DATE/TIME NOTARIZED:	DOCUMENT DATE:	FEE CHARGED:
COMMENTS:			RECORD NUMBER: **73**

NOTARY RECORD

FULL NAME:	EMAIL:	THUMB PRINT
PHONE NUMBER:	SIGNER'S SIGNATURE:	
ADDRESS:		

SERVICES PROVIDED:	IDENTIFICATION:		ID NUMBER:
☐ JURAT	☐ ID CARD	☐ CREDIBLE WITNESS	
☐ OATH	☐ PASSPORT	☐ KNOWN PERSONALLY	ISSUED BY:
☐ ACKNOWLEDGEMENT	☐ DRIVERS LICENSE		DATE ISSUE : / EXPIRATION DATE:
☐ OTHER :	☐ OTHER :		

WITNESS FULL NAME:	EMAIL:
PHONE NUMBER:	WITNESS SIGNATURE:
ADDRESS:	

DOCUMENT TYPE:	DATE/TIME NOTARIZED:	DOCUMENT DATE:	FEE CHARGED:
COMMENTS:			RECORD NUMBER: **74**

NOTARY RECORD

FULL NAME:	EMAIL:	THUMB PRINT
PHONE NUMBER:	SIGNER'S SIGNATURE:	
ADDRESS:		

SERVICES PROVIDED:	IDENTIFICATION:		ID NUMBER:	
☐ JURAT	☐ ID CARD	☐ CREDIBLE WITNESS		
☐ OATH	☐ PASSPORT	☐ KNOWN PERSONALLY	ISSUED BY:	
☐ ACKNOWLEDGEMENT	☐ DRIVERS LICENSE		DATE ISSUE :	EXPIRATION DATE:
☐ OTHER :	☐ OTHER :			

WITNESS FULL NAME:	EMAIL:
PHONE NUMBER:	WITNESS SIGNATURE:
ADDRESS:	

DOCUMENT TYPE:	DATE/TIME NOTARIZED:	DOCUMENT DATE:	FEE CHARGED:
COMMENTS:			RECORD NUMBER: 75

NOTARY RECORD

FULL NAME:	EMAIL:	THUMB PRINT
PHONE NUMBER:	SIGNER'S SIGNATURE:	
ADDRESS:		

SERVICES PROVIDED:	IDENTIFICATION:		ID NUMBER:	
☐ JURAT	☐ ID CARD	☐ CREDIBLE WITNESS		
☐ OATH	☐ PASSPORT	☐ KNOWN PERSONALLY	ISSUED BY:	
☐ ACKNOWLEDGEMENT	☐ DRIVERS LICENSE		DATE ISSUE :	EXPIRATION DATE:
☐ OTHER :	☐ OTHER :			

WITNESS FULL NAME:	EMAIL:
PHONE NUMBER:	WITNESS SIGNATURE:
ADDRESS:	

DOCUMENT TYPE:	DATE/TIME NOTARIZED:	DOCUMENT DATE:	FEE CHARGED:
COMMENTS:			RECORD NUMBER: 76

NOTARY RECORD

FULL NAME:	EMAIL:	THUMB PRINT
PHONE NUMBER:	SIGNER'S SIGNATURE:	
ADDRESS:		

SERVICES PROVIDED:
- ☐ JURAT
- ☐ OATH
- ☐ ACKNOWLEDGEMENT
- ☐ OTHER : ....

IDENTIFICATION:
- ☐ ID CARD
- ☐ PASSPORT
- ☐ DRIVERS LICENSE
- ☐ OTHER : ....
- ☐ CREDIBLE WITNESS
- ☐ KNOWN PERSONALLY

ID NUMBER:
ISSUED BY:
DATE ISSUE :	EXPIRATION DATE:

WITNESS FULL NAME:	EMAIL:
PHONE NUMBER:	WITNESS SIGNATURE:
ADDRESS:	

DOCUMENT TYPE:	DATE/TIME NOTARIZED:	DOCUMENT DATE:	FEE CHARGED:
COMMENTS:			RECORD NUMBER: **77**

NOTARY RECORD

FULL NAME:	EMAIL:	THUMB PRINT
PHONE NUMBER:	SIGNER'S SIGNATURE:	
ADDRESS:		

SERVICES PROVIDED:
- ☐ JURAT
- ☐ OATH
- ☐ ACKNOWLEDGEMENT
- ☐ OTHER : ....

IDENTIFICATION:
- ☐ ID CARD
- ☐ PASSPORT
- ☐ DRIVERS LICENSE
- ☐ OTHER : ....
- ☐ CREDIBLE WITNESS
- ☐ KNOWN PERSONALLY

ID NUMBER:
ISSUED BY:
DATE ISSUE :	EXPIRATION DATE:

WITNESS FULL NAME:	EMAIL:
PHONE NUMBER:	WITNESS SIGNATURE:
ADDRESS:	

DOCUMENT TYPE:	DATE/TIME NOTARIZED:	DOCUMENT DATE:	FEE CHARGED:
COMMENTS:			RECORD NUMBER: **78**

NOTARY RECORD

FULL NAME:	EMAIL:	THUMB PRINT
PHONE NUMBER:	SIGNER'S SIGNATURE:	
ADDRESS:		

SERVICES PROVIDED:	IDENTIFICATION:		ID NUMBER:
☐ JURAT	☐ ID CARD	☐ CREDIBLE WITNESS	
☐ OATH	☐ PASSPORT	☐ KNOWN PERSONALLY	ISSUED BY:
☐ ACKNOWLEDGEMENT	☐ DRIVERS LICENSE		DATE ISSUE : / EXPIRATION DATE:
☐ OTHER :	☐ OTHER :		

WITNESS FULL NAME:	EMAIL:
PHONE NUMBER:	WITNESS SIGNATURE:
ADDRESS:	

DOCUMENT TYPE:	DATE/TIME NOTARIZED:	DOCUMENT DATE:	FEE CHARGED:

COMMENTS:	RECORD NUMBER: **79**

NOTARY RECORD

FULL NAME:	EMAIL:	THUMB PRINT
PHONE NUMBER:	SIGNER'S SIGNATURE:	
ADDRESS:		

SERVICES PROVIDED:	IDENTIFICATION:		ID NUMBER:
☐ JURAT	☐ ID CARD	☐ CREDIBLE WITNESS	
☐ OATH	☐ PASSPORT	☐ KNOWN PERSONALLY	ISSUED BY:
☐ ACKNOWLEDGEMENT	☐ DRIVERS LICENSE		DATE ISSUE : / EXPIRATION DATE:
☐ OTHER :	☐ OTHER :		

WITNESS FULL NAME:	EMAIL:
PHONE NUMBER:	WITNESS SIGNATURE:
ADDRESS:	

DOCUMENT TYPE:	DATE/TIME NOTARIZED:	DOCUMENT DATE:	FEE CHARGED:

COMMENTS:	RECORD NUMBER: **80**

NOTARY RECORD

FULL NAME:	EMAIL:	THUMB PRINT
PHONE NUMBER:	SIGNER'S SIGNATURE:	
ADDRESS:		

SERVICES PROVIDED:	IDENTIFICATION:		ID NUMBER:
☐ JURAT	☐ ID CARD	☐ CREDIBLE WITNESS	
☐ OATH	☐ PASSPORT	☐ KNOWN PERSONALLY	ISSUED BY:
☐ ACKNOWLEDGEMENT	☐ DRIVERS LICENSE		DATE ISSUE : / EXPIRATION DATE:
☐ OTHER :	☐ OTHER :		

WITNESS FULL NAME:	EMAIL:
PHONE NUMBER:	WITNESS SIGNATURE:
ADDRESS:	

DOCUMENT TYPE:	DATE/TIME NOTARIZED:	DOCUMENT DATE:	FEE CHARGED:

COMMENTS:	RECORD NUMBER: 81

NOTARY RECORD

FULL NAME:	EMAIL:	THUMB PRINT
PHONE NUMBER:	SIGNER'S SIGNATURE:	
ADDRESS:		

SERVICES PROVIDED:	IDENTIFICATION:		ID NUMBER:
☐ JURAT	☐ ID CARD	☐ CREDIBLE WITNESS	
☐ OATH	☐ PASSPORT	☐ KNOWN PERSONALLY	ISSUED BY:
☐ ACKNOWLEDGEMENT	☐ DRIVERS LICENSE		DATE ISSUE : / EXPIRATION DATE:
☐ OTHER :	☐ OTHER :		

WITNESS FULL NAME:	EMAIL:
PHONE NUMBER:	WITNESS SIGNATURE:
ADDRESS:	

DOCUMENT TYPE:	DATE/TIME NOTARIZED:	DOCUMENT DATE:	FEE CHARGED:

COMMENTS:	RECORD NUMBER: 82

NOTARY RECORD

FULL NAME:	EMAIL:	THUMB PRINT
PHONE NUMBER:	SIGNER'S SIGNATURE:	
ADDRESS:		

SERVICES PROVIDED:	IDENTIFICATION:		ID NUMBER:
☐ JURAT	☐ ID CARD	☐ CREDIBLE WITNESS	
☐ OATH	☐ PASSPORT	☐ KNOWN PERSONALLY	ISSUED BY:
☐ ACKNOWLEDGEMENT	☐ DRIVERS LICENSE		DATE ISSUE : / EXPIRATION DATE:
☐ OTHER :	☐ OTHER :		

WITNESS FULL NAME:	EMAIL:
PHONE NUMBER:	WITNESS SIGNATURE:
ADDRESS:	

DOCUMENT TYPE:	DATE/TIME NOTARIZED:	DOCUMENT DATE:	FEE CHARGED:
COMMENTS:			RECORD NUMBER: 83

NOTARY RECORD

FULL NAME:	EMAIL:	THUMB PRINT
PHONE NUMBER:	SIGNER'S SIGNATURE:	
ADDRESS:		

SERVICES PROVIDED:	IDENTIFICATION:		ID NUMBER:
☐ JURAT	☐ ID CARD	☐ CREDIBLE WITNESS	
☐ OATH	☐ PASSPORT	☐ KNOWN PERSONALLY	ISSUED BY:
☐ ACKNOWLEDGEMENT	☐ DRIVERS LICENSE		DATE ISSUE : / EXPIRATION DATE:
☐ OTHER :	☐ OTHER :		

WITNESS FULL NAME:	EMAIL:
PHONE NUMBER:	WITNESS SIGNATURE:
ADDRESS:	

DOCUMENT TYPE:	DATE/TIME NOTARIZED:	DOCUMENT DATE:	FEE CHARGED:
COMMENTS:			RECORD NUMBER: 84

NOTARY RECORD

FULL NAME:

EMAIL:

THUMB PRINT

PHONE NUMBER:

SIGNER'S SIGNATURE:

ADDRESS:

SERVICES PROVIDED:
- ☐ JURAT
- ☐ OATH
- ☐ ACKNOWLEDGEMENT
- ☐ OTHER : ....

IDENTIFICATION:
- ☐ ID CARD
- ☐ PASSPORT
- ☐ DRIVERS LICENSE
- ☐ OTHER : ....

- ☐ CREDIBLE WITNESS
- ☐ KNOWN PERSONALLY

ID NUMBER:

ISSUED BY:

DATE ISSUE :

EXPIRATION DATE:

WITNESS FULL NAME:

EMAIL:

PHONE NUMBER:

WITNESS SIGNATURE:

ADDRESS:

DOCUMENT TYPE:	DATE/TIME NOTARIZED:	DOCUMENT DATE:	FEE CHARGED:

COMMENTS:

RECORD NUMBER: 85

NOTARY RECORD

FULL NAME:

EMAIL:

THUMB PRINT

PHONE NUMBER:

SIGNER'S SIGNATURE:

ADDRESS:

SERVICES PROVIDED:
- ☐ JURAT
- ☐ OATH
- ☐ ACKNOWLEDGEMENT
- ☐ OTHER : ....

IDENTIFICATION:
- ☐ ID CARD
- ☐ PASSPORT
- ☐ DRIVERS LICENSE
- ☐ OTHER : ....

- ☐ CREDIBLE WITNESS
- ☐ KNOWN PERSONALLY

ID NUMBER:

ISSUED BY:

DATE ISSUE :

EXPIRATION DATE:

WITNESS FULL NAME:

EMAIL:

PHONE NUMBER:

WITNESS SIGNATURE:

ADDRESS:

DOCUMENT TYPE:	DATE/TIME NOTARIZED:	DOCUMENT DATE:	FEE CHARGED:

COMMENTS:

RECORD NUMBER: 86

NOTARY RECORD

FULL NAME:

EMAIL:

THUMB PRINT

PHONE NUMBER:

SIGNER'S SIGNATURE:

ADDRESS:

SERVICES PROVIDED:
- ☐ JURAT
- ☐ OATH
- ☐ ACKNOWLEDGEMENT
- ☐ OTHER : ....

IDENTIFICATION:
- ☐ ID CARD
- ☐ PASSPORT
- ☐ DRIVERS LICENSE
- ☐ OTHER : ....

- ☐ CREDIBLE WITNESS
- ☐ KNOWN PERSONALLY

ID NUMBER:

ISSUED BY:

DATE ISSUE :

EXPIRATION DATE:

WITNESS FULL NAME:

EMAIL:

PHONE NUMBER:

WITNESS SIGNATURE:

ADDRESS:

DOCUMENT TYPE:

DATE/TIME NOTARIZED:

DOCUMENT DATE:

FEE CHARGED:

COMMENTS:

RECORD NUMBER: **87**

NOTARY RECORD

FULL NAME:

EMAIL:

THUMB PRINT

PHONE NUMBER:

SIGNER'S SIGNATURE:

ADDRESS:

SERVICES PROVIDED:
- ☐ JURAT
- ☐ OATH
- ☐ ACKNOWLEDGEMENT
- ☐ OTHER : ....

IDENTIFICATION:
- ☐ ID CARD
- ☐ PASSPORT
- ☐ DRIVERS LICENSE
- ☐ OTHER : ....

- ☐ CREDIBLE WITNESS
- ☐ KNOWN PERSONALLY

ID NUMBER:

ISSUED BY:

DATE ISSUE :

EXPIRATION DATE:

WITNESS FULL NAME:

EMAIL:

PHONE NUMBER:

WITNESS SIGNATURE:

ADDRESS:

DOCUMENT TYPE:

DATE/TIME NOTARIZED:

DOCUMENT DATE:

FEE CHARGED:

COMMENTS:

RECORD NUMBER: **88**

NOTARY RECORD

FULL NAME:

EMAIL:

THUMB PRINT

PHONE NUMBER:

SIGNER'S SIGNATURE:

ADDRESS:

SERVICES PROVIDED:	IDENTIFICATION:		
☐ JURAT	☐ ID CARD	☐ CREDIBLE WITNESS	**ID NUMBER:**
☐ OATH	☐ PASSPORT	☐ KNOWN PERSONALLY	**ISSUED BY:**
☐ ACKNOWLEDGEMENT	☐ DRIVERS LICENSE		**DATE ISSUE :** / **EXPIRATION DATE:**
☐ OTHER :	☐ OTHER :		

WITNESS FULL NAME:

EMAIL:

PHONE NUMBER:

WITNESS SIGNATURE:

ADDRESS:

DOCUMENT TYPE:	DATE/TIME NOTARIZED:	DOCUMENT DATE:	FEE CHARGED:

COMMENTS:

RECORD NUMBER: **89**

NOTARY RECORD

FULL NAME:

EMAIL:

THUMB PRINT

PHONE NUMBER:

SIGNER'S SIGNATURE:

ADDRESS:

SERVICES PROVIDED:	IDENTIFICATION:		
☐ JURAT	☐ ID CARD	☐ CREDIBLE WITNESS	**ID NUMBER:**
☐ OATH	☐ PASSPORT	☐ KNOWN PERSONALLY	**ISSUED BY:**
☐ ACKNOWLEDGEMENT	☐ DRIVERS LICENSE		**DATE ISSUE :** / **EXPIRATION DATE:**
☐ OTHER :	☐ OTHER :		

WITNESS FULL NAME:

EMAIL:

PHONE NUMBER:

WITNESS SIGNATURE:

ADDRESS:

DOCUMENT TYPE:	DATE/TIME NOTARIZED:	DOCUMENT DATE:	FEE CHARGED:

COMMENTS:

RECORD NUMBER: **90**

NOTARY RECORD

FULL NAME:	EMAIL:	THUMB PRINT
PHONE NUMBER:	SIGNER'S SIGNATURE:	
ADDRESS:		

SERVICES PROVIDED:	IDENTIFICATION:		ID NUMBER:
☐ JURAT	☐ ID CARD	☐ CREDIBLE WITNESS	
☐ OATH	☐ PASSPORT	☐ KNOWN PERSONALLY	ISSUED BY:
☐ ACKNOWLEDGEMENT	☐ DRIVERS LICENSE		DATE ISSUE : / EXPIRATION DATE:
☐ OTHER :	☐ OTHER :		

WITNESS FULL NAME:	EMAIL:
PHONE NUMBER:	WITNESS SIGNATURE:
ADDRESS:	

DOCUMENT TYPE:	DATE/TIME NOTARIZED:	DOCUMENT DATE:	FEE CHARGED:

COMMENTS:	RECORD NUMBER: 91

NOTARY RECORD

FULL NAME:	EMAIL:	THUMB PRINT
PHONE NUMBER:	SIGNER'S SIGNATURE:	
ADDRESS:		

SERVICES PROVIDED:	IDENTIFICATION:		ID NUMBER:
☐ JURAT	☐ ID CARD	☐ CREDIBLE WITNESS	
☐ OATH	☐ PASSPORT	☐ KNOWN PERSONALLY	ISSUED BY:
☐ ACKNOWLEDGEMENT	☐ DRIVERS LICENSE		DATE ISSUE : / EXPIRATION DATE:
☐ OTHER :	☐ OTHER :		

WITNESS FULL NAME:	EMAIL:
PHONE NUMBER:	WITNESS SIGNATURE:
ADDRESS:	

DOCUMENT TYPE:	DATE/TIME NOTARIZED:	DOCUMENT DATE:	FEE CHARGED:

COMMENTS:	RECORD NUMBER: 92

NOTARY RECORD

FULL NAME:

EMAIL:

THUMB PRINT

PHONE NUMBER:

SIGNER'S SIGNATURE:

ADDRESS:

SERVICES PROVIDED:
- ☐ JURAT
- ☐ OATH
- ☐ ACKNOWLEDGEMENT
- ☐ OTHER : ....

IDENTIFICATION:
- ☐ ID CARD
- ☐ PASSPORT
- ☐ DRIVERS LICENSE
- ☐ OTHER : ....

- ☐ CREDIBLE WITNESS
- ☐ KNOWN PERSONALLY

ID NUMBER:

ISSUED BY:

DATE ISSUE :

EXPIRATION DATE:

WITNESS FULL NAME:

EMAIL:

PHONE NUMBER:

WITNESS SIGNATURE:

ADDRESS:

DOCUMENT TYPE:

DATE/TIME NOTARIZED:

DOCUMENT DATE:

FEE CHARGED:

COMMENTS:

RECORD NUMBER: 93

NOTARY RECORD

FULL NAME:

EMAIL:

THUMB PRINT

PHONE NUMBER:

SIGNER'S SIGNATURE:

ADDRESS:

SERVICES PROVIDED:
- ☐ JURAT
- ☐ OATH
- ☐ ACKNOWLEDGEMENT
- ☐ OTHER : ....

IDENTIFICATION:
- ☐ ID CARD
- ☐ PASSPORT
- ☐ DRIVERS LICENSE
- ☐ OTHER : ....

- ☐ CREDIBLE WITNESS
- ☐ KNOWN PERSONALLY

ID NUMBER:

ISSUED BY:

DATE ISSUE :

EXPIRATION DATE:

WITNESS FULL NAME:

EMAIL:

PHONE NUMBER:

WITNESS SIGNATURE:

ADDRESS:

DOCUMENT TYPE:

DATE/TIME NOTARIZED:

DOCUMENT DATE:

FEE CHARGED:

COMMENTS:

RECORD NUMBER: 94

NOTARY RECORD

FULL NAME:	EMAIL:	THUMB PRINT
PHONE NUMBER:	SIGNER'S SIGNATURE:	
ADDRESS:		

SERVICES PROVIDED:	IDENTIFICATION:		ID NUMBER:
☐ JURAT	☐ ID CARD	☐ CREDIBLE WITNESS	
☐ OATH	☐ PASSPORT	☐ KNOWN PERSONALLY	ISSUED BY:
☐ ACKNOWLEDGEMENT	☐ DRIVERS LICENSE		DATE ISSUE :
☐ OTHER :	☐ OTHER :		EXPIRATION DATE:

WITNESS FULL NAME:	EMAIL:
PHONE NUMBER:	WITNESS SIGNATURE:
ADDRESS:	

DOCUMENT TYPE:	DATE/TIME NOTARIZED:	DOCUMENT DATE:	FEE CHARGED:
COMMENTS:			RECORD NUMBER: **95**

NOTARY RECORD

FULL NAME:	EMAIL:	THUMB PRINT
PHONE NUMBER:	SIGNER'S SIGNATURE:	
ADDRESS:		

SERVICES PROVIDED:	IDENTIFICATION:		ID NUMBER:
☐ JURAT	☐ ID CARD	☐ CREDIBLE WITNESS	
☐ OATH	☐ PASSPORT	☐ KNOWN PERSONALLY	ISSUED BY:
☐ ACKNOWLEDGEMENT	☐ DRIVERS LICENSE		DATE ISSUE :
☐ OTHER :	☐ OTHER :		EXPIRATION DATE:

WITNESS FULL NAME:	EMAIL:
PHONE NUMBER:	WITNESS SIGNATURE:
ADDRESS:	

DOCUMENT TYPE:	DATE/TIME NOTARIZED:	DOCUMENT DATE:	FEE CHARGED:
COMMENTS:			RECORD NUMBER: **96**

NOTARY RECORD

FULL NAME:

EMAIL:

THUMB PRINT

PHONE NUMBER:

SIGNER'S SIGNATURE:

ADDRESS:

SERVICES PROVIDED:

- ☐ JURAT
- ☐ OATH
- ☐ ACKNOWLEDGEMENT
- ☐ OTHER : ....

IDENTIFICATION:

- ☐ ID CARD
- ☐ PASSPORT
- ☐ DRIVERS LICENSE
- ☐ OTHER : ....

- ☐ CREDIBLE WITNESS
- ☐ KNOWN PERSONALLY

ID NUMBER:

ISSUED BY:

DATE ISSUE :

EXPIRATION DATE:

WITNESS FULL NAME:

EMAIL:

PHONE NUMBER:

WITNESS SIGNATURE:

ADDRESS:

DOCUMENT TYPE:	DATE/TIME NOTARIZED:	DOCUMENT DATE:	FEE CHARGED:

COMMENTS:

RECORD NUMBER: 97

NOTARY RECORD

FULL NAME:

EMAIL:

THUMB PRINT

PHONE NUMBER:

SIGNER'S SIGNATURE:

ADDRESS:

SERVICES PROVIDED:

- ☐ JURAT
- ☐ OATH
- ☐ ACKNOWLEDGEMENT
- ☐ OTHER : ....

IDENTIFICATION:

- ☐ ID CARD
- ☐ PASSPORT
- ☐ DRIVERS LICENSE
- ☐ OTHER : ....

- ☐ CREDIBLE WITNESS
- ☐ KNOWN PERSONALLY

ID NUMBER:

ISSUED BY:

DATE ISSUE :

EXPIRATION DATE:

WITNESS FULL NAME:

EMAIL:

PHONE NUMBER:

WITNESS SIGNATURE:

ADDRESS:

DOCUMENT TYPE:	DATE/TIME NOTARIZED:	DOCUMENT DATE:	FEE CHARGED:

COMMENTS:

RECORD NUMBER: 98

NOTARY RECORD

FULL NAME:	EMAIL:	THUMB PRINT
PHONE NUMBER:	SIGNER'S SIGNATURE:	
ADDRESS:		

SERVICES PROVIDED:	IDENTIFICATION:		ID NUMBER:
☐ JURAT	☐ ID CARD	☐ CREDIBLE WITNESS	
☐ OATH	☐ PASSPORT	☐ KNOWN PERSONALLY	ISSUED BY:
☐ ACKNOWLEDGEMENT	☐ DRIVERS LICENSE		DATE ISSUE :
☐ OTHER :	☐ OTHER :		EXPIRATION DATE:

WITNESS FULL NAME:	EMAIL:
PHONE NUMBER:	WITNESS SIGNATURE:
ADDRESS:	

DOCUMENT TYPE:	DATE/TIME NOTARIZED:	DOCUMENT DATE:	FEE CHARGED:
COMMENTS:		RECORD NUMBER:	99

NOTARY RECORD

FULL NAME:	EMAIL:	THUMB PRINT
PHONE NUMBER:	SIGNER'S SIGNATURE:	
ADDRESS:		

SERVICES PROVIDED:	IDENTIFICATION:		ID NUMBER:
☐ JURAT	☐ ID CARD	☐ CREDIBLE WITNESS	
☐ OATH	☐ PASSPORT	☐ KNOWN PERSONALLY	ISSUED BY:
☐ ACKNOWLEDGEMENT	☐ DRIVERS LICENSE		DATE ISSUE :
☐ OTHER :	☐ OTHER :		EXPIRATION DATE:

WITNESS FULL NAME:	EMAIL:
PHONE NUMBER:	WITNESS SIGNATURE:
ADDRESS:	

DOCUMENT TYPE:	DATE/TIME NOTARIZED:	DOCUMENT DATE:	FEE CHARGED:
COMMENTS:		RECORD NUMBER:	100

NOTARY RECORD

FULL NAME:

EMAIL:

THUMB PRINT

PHONE NUMBER:

SIGNER'S SIGNATURE:

ADDRESS:

SERVICES PROVIDED:

- ☐ JURAT
- ☐ OATH
- ☐ ACKNOWLEDGEMENT
- ☐ OTHER : ....

IDENTIFICATION:

- ☐ ID CARD
- ☐ PASSPORT
- ☐ DRIVERS LICENSE
- ☐ OTHER : ....

- ☐ CREDIBLE WITNESS
- ☐ KNOWN PERSONALLY

ID NUMBER:

ISSUED BY:

DATE ISSUE :

EXPIRATION DATE:

WITNESS FULL NAME:

EMAIL:

PHONE NUMBER:

WITNESS SIGNATURE:

ADDRESS:

DOCUMENT TYPE:	DATE/TIME NOTARIZED:	DOCUMENT DATE:	FEE CHARGED:

COMMENTS:

RECORD NUMBER: **101**

NOTARY RECORD

FULL NAME:

EMAIL:

THUMB PRINT

PHONE NUMBER:

SIGNER'S SIGNATURE:

ADDRESS:

SERVICES PROVIDED:

- ☐ JURAT
- ☐ OATH
- ☐ ACKNOWLEDGEMENT
- ☐ OTHER : ....

IDENTIFICATION:

- ☐ ID CARD
- ☐ PASSPORT
- ☐ DRIVERS LICENSE
- ☐ OTHER : ....

- ☐ CREDIBLE WITNESS
- ☐ KNOWN PERSONALLY

ID NUMBER:

ISSUED BY:

DATE ISSUE :

EXPIRATION DATE:

WITNESS FULL NAME:

EMAIL:

PHONE NUMBER:

WITNESS SIGNATURE:

ADDRESS:

DOCUMENT TYPE:	DATE/TIME NOTARIZED:	DOCUMENT DATE:	FEE CHARGED:

COMMENTS:

RECORD NUMBER: **102**

NOTARY RECORD

FULL NAME:

EMAIL:

THUMB PRINT

PHONE NUMBER:

SIGNER'S SIGNATURE:

ADDRESS:

SERVICES PROVIDED:
- ☐ JURAT
- ☐ OATH
- ☐ ACKNOWLEDGEMENT
- ☐ OTHER : ....

IDENTIFICATION:
- ☐ ID CARD
- ☐ PASSPORT
- ☐ DRIVERS LICENSE
- ☐ OTHER : ....

- ☐ CREDIBLE WITNESS
- ☐ KNOWN PERSONALLY

ID NUMBER:

ISSUED BY:

DATE ISSUE :

EXPIRATION DATE:

WITNESS FULL NAME:

EMAIL:

PHONE NUMBER:

WITNESS SIGNATURE:

ADDRESS:

DOCUMENT TYPE:

DATE/TIME NOTARIZED:

DOCUMENT DATE:

FEE CHARGED:

COMMENTS:

RECORD NUMBER: **103**

NOTARY RECORD

FULL NAME:

EMAIL:

THUMB PRINT

PHONE NUMBER:

SIGNER'S SIGNATURE:

ADDRESS:

SERVICES PROVIDED:
- ☐ JURAT
- ☐ OATH
- ☐ ACKNOWLEDGEMENT
- ☐ OTHER : ....

IDENTIFICATION:
- ☐ ID CARD
- ☐ PASSPORT
- ☐ DRIVERS LICENSE
- ☐ OTHER : ....

- ☐ CREDIBLE WITNESS
- ☐ KNOWN PERSONALLY

ID NUMBER:

ISSUED BY:

DATE ISSUE :

EXPIRATION DATE:

WITNESS FULL NAME:

EMAIL:

PHONE NUMBER:

WITNESS SIGNATURE:

ADDRESS:

DOCUMENT TYPE:

DATE/TIME NOTARIZED:

DOCUMENT DATE:

FEE CHARGED:

COMMENTS:

RECORD NUMBER: **104**

NOTARY RECORD

FULL NAME:	EMAIL:	THUMB PRINT
PHONE NUMBER:	SIGNER'S SIGNATURE:	
ADDRESS:		

SERVICES PROVIDED:	IDENTIFICATION:		ID NUMBER:
☐ JURAT	☐ ID CARD	☐ CREDIBLE WITNESS	
☐ OATH	☐ PASSPORT	☐ KNOWN PERSONALLY	ISSUED BY:
☐ ACKNOWLEDGEMENT	☐ DRIVERS LICENSE		DATE ISSUE : / EXPIRATION DATE:
☐ OTHER :	☐ OTHER :		

WITNESS FULL NAME:	EMAIL:
PHONE NUMBER:	WITNESS SIGNATURE:
ADDRESS:	

DOCUMENT TYPE:	DATE/TIME NOTARIZED:	DOCUMENT DATE:	FEE CHARGED:
COMMENTS:			RECORD NUMBER: **105**

NOTARY RECORD

FULL NAME:	EMAIL:	THUMB PRINT
PHONE NUMBER:	SIGNER'S SIGNATURE:	
ADDRESS:		

SERVICES PROVIDED:	IDENTIFICATION:		ID NUMBER:
☐ JURAT	☐ ID CARD	☐ CREDIBLE WITNESS	
☐ OATH	☐ PASSPORT	☐ KNOWN PERSONALLY	ISSUED BY:
☐ ACKNOWLEDGEMENT	☐ DRIVERS LICENSE		DATE ISSUE : / EXPIRATION DATE:
☐ OTHER :	☐ OTHER :		

WITNESS FULL NAME:	EMAIL:
PHONE NUMBER:	WITNESS SIGNATURE:
ADDRESS:	

DOCUMENT TYPE:	DATE/TIME NOTARIZED:	DOCUMENT DATE:	FEE CHARGED:
COMMENTS:			RECORD NUMBER: **106**

NOTARY RECORD

FULL NAME:	EMAIL:	THUMB PRINT
PHONE NUMBER:	SIGNER'S SIGNATURE:	
ADDRESS:		

SERVICES PROVIDED:	IDENTIFICATION:		ID NUMBER:
☐ JURAT	☐ ID CARD	☐ CREDIBLE WITNESS	
☐ OATH	☐ PASSPORT	☐ KNOWN PERSONALLY	ISSUED BY:
☐ ACKNOWLEDGEMENT	☐ DRIVERS LICENSE		DATE ISSUE : / EXPIRATION DATE:
☐ OTHER :	☐ OTHER :		

WITNESS FULL NAME:	EMAIL:
PHONE NUMBER:	WITNESS SIGNATURE:
ADDRESS:	

DOCUMENT TYPE:	DATE/TIME NOTARIZED:	DOCUMENT DATE:	FEE CHARGED:

COMMENTS:	RECORD NUMBER: 107

NOTARY RECORD

FULL NAME:	EMAIL:	THUMB PRINT
PHONE NUMBER:	SIGNER'S SIGNATURE:	
ADDRESS:		

SERVICES PROVIDED:	IDENTIFICATION:		ID NUMBER:
☐ JURAT	☐ ID CARD	☐ CREDIBLE WITNESS	
☐ OATH	☐ PASSPORT	☐ KNOWN PERSONALLY	ISSUED BY:
☐ ACKNOWLEDGEMENT	☐ DRIVERS LICENSE		DATE ISSUE : / EXPIRATION DATE:
☐ OTHER :	☐ OTHER :		

WITNESS FULL NAME:	EMAIL:
PHONE NUMBER:	WITNESS SIGNATURE:
ADDRESS:	

DOCUMENT TYPE:	DATE/TIME NOTARIZED:	DOCUMENT DATE:	FEE CHARGED:

COMMENTS:	RECORD NUMBER: 108

NOTARY RECORD

FULL NAME:

EMAIL:

THUMB PRINT

PHONE NUMBER:

SIGNER'S SIGNATURE:

ADDRESS:

SERVICES PROVIDED:	IDENTIFICATION:		ID NUMBER:
☐ JURAT	☐ ID CARD	☐ CREDIBLE WITNESS	
☐ OATH	☐ PASSPORT	☐ KNOWN PERSONALLY	ISSUED BY:
☐ ACKNOWLEDGEMENT	☐ DRIVERS LICENSE		DATE ISSUE : / EXPIRATION DATE:
☐ OTHER :	☐ OTHER :		

WITNESS FULL NAME:

EMAIL:

PHONE NUMBER:

WITNESS SIGNATURE:

ADDRESS:

DOCUMENT TYPE:	DATE/TIME NOTARIZED:	DOCUMENT DATE:	FEE CHARGED:

COMMENTS:

RECORD NUMBER: **109**

NOTARY RECORD

FULL NAME:

EMAIL:

THUMB PRINT

PHONE NUMBER:

SIGNER'S SIGNATURE:

ADDRESS:

SERVICES PROVIDED:	IDENTIFICATION:		ID NUMBER:
☐ JURAT	☐ ID CARD	☐ CREDIBLE WITNESS	
☐ OATH	☐ PASSPORT	☐ KNOWN PERSONALLY	ISSUED BY:
☐ ACKNOWLEDGEMENT	☐ DRIVERS LICENSE		DATE ISSUE : / EXPIRATION DATE:
☐ OTHER :	☐ OTHER :		

WITNESS FULL NAME:

EMAIL:

PHONE NUMBER:

WITNESS SIGNATURE:

ADDRESS:

DOCUMENT TYPE:	DATE/TIME NOTARIZED:	DOCUMENT DATE:	FEE CHARGED:

COMMENTS:

RECORD NUMBER: **110**

NOTARY RECORD

FULL NAME:	EMAIL:	THUMB PRINT
PHONE NUMBER:	SIGNER'S SIGNATURE:	
ADDRESS:		

SERVICES PROVIDED:	IDENTIFICATION:		ID NUMBER:
☐ JURAT	☐ ID CARD	☐ CREDIBLE WITNESS	
☐ OATH	☐ PASSPORT	☐ KNOWN PERSONALLY	ISSUED BY:
☐ ACKNOWLEDGEMENT	☐ DRIVERS LICENSE		DATE ISSUE : / EXPIRATION DATE:
☐ OTHER :	☐ OTHER :		

WITNESS FULL NAME:	EMAIL:
PHONE NUMBER:	WITNESS SIGNATURE:
ADDRESS:	

DOCUMENT TYPE:	DATE/TIME NOTARIZED:	DOCUMENT DATE:	FEE CHARGED:

COMMENTS:	RECORD NUMBER: **111**

NOTARY RECORD

FULL NAME:	EMAIL:	THUMB PRINT
PHONE NUMBER:	SIGNER'S SIGNATURE:	
ADDRESS:		

SERVICES PROVIDED:	IDENTIFICATION:		ID NUMBER:
☐ JURAT	☐ ID CARD	☐ CREDIBLE WITNESS	
☐ OATH	☐ PASSPORT	☐ KNOWN PERSONALLY	ISSUED BY:
☐ ACKNOWLEDGEMENT	☐ DRIVERS LICENSE		DATE ISSUE : / EXPIRATION DATE:
☐ OTHER :	☐ OTHER :		

WITNESS FULL NAME:	EMAIL:
PHONE NUMBER:	WITNESS SIGNATURE:
ADDRESS:	

DOCUMENT TYPE:	DATE/TIME NOTARIZED:	DOCUMENT DATE:	FEE CHARGED:

COMMENTS:	RECORD NUMBER: **112**

NOTARY RECORD

FULL NAME:

EMAIL:

THUMB PRINT

PHONE NUMBER:

SIGNER'S SIGNATURE:

ADDRESS:

SERVICES PROVIDED:	IDENTIFICATION:		
☐ JURAT	☐ ID CARD	☐ CREDIBLE WITNESS	**ID NUMBER:**
☐ OATH	☐ PASSPORT	☐ KNOWN PERSONALLY	**ISSUED BY:**
☐ ACKNOWLEDGEMENT	☐ DRIVERS LICENSE		**DATE ISSUE :** / **EXPIRATION DATE:**
☐ OTHER :	☐ OTHER :		

WITNESS FULL NAME:

EMAIL:

PHONE NUMBER:

WITNESS SIGNATURE:

ADDRESS:

DOCUMENT TYPE:	DATE/TIME NOTARIZED:	DOCUMENT DATE:	FEE CHARGED:

COMMENTS:

RECORD NUMBER: **113**

NOTARY RECORD

FULL NAME:

EMAIL:

THUMB PRINT

PHONE NUMBER:

SIGNER'S SIGNATURE:

ADDRESS:

SERVICES PROVIDED:	IDENTIFICATION:		
☐ JURAT	☐ ID CARD	☐ CREDIBLE WITNESS	**ID NUMBER:**
☐ OATH	☐ PASSPORT	☐ KNOWN PERSONALLY	**ISSUED BY:**
☐ ACKNOWLEDGEMENT	☐ DRIVERS LICENSE		**DATE ISSUE :** / **EXPIRATION DATE:**
☐ OTHER :	☐ OTHER :		

WITNESS FULL NAME:

EMAIL:

PHONE NUMBER:

WITNESS SIGNATURE:

ADDRESS:

DOCUMENT TYPE:	DATE/TIME NOTARIZED:	DOCUMENT DATE:	FEE CHARGED:

COMMENTS:

RECORD NUMBER: **114**

NOTARY RECORD

FULL NAME:	EMAIL:	THUMB PRINT
PHONE NUMBER:	SIGNER'S SIGNATURE:	
ADDRESS:		

SERVICES PROVIDED:	IDENTIFICATION:		ID NUMBER:
☐ JURAT	☐ ID CARD	☐ CREDIBLE WITNESS	
☐ OATH	☐ PASSPORT	☐ KNOWN PERSONALLY	ISSUED BY:
☐ ACKNOWLEDGEMENT	☐ DRIVERS LICENSE		DATE ISSUE : / EXPIRATION DATE:
☐ OTHER :	☐ OTHER :		

WITNESS FULL NAME:	EMAIL:
PHONE NUMBER:	WITNESS SIGNATURE:
ADDRESS:	

DOCUMENT TYPE:	DATE/TIME NOTARIZED:	DOCUMENT DATE:	FEE CHARGED:

COMMENTS:	RECORD NUMBER: 115

NOTARY RECORD

FULL NAME:	EMAIL:	THUMB PRINT
PHONE NUMBER:	SIGNER'S SIGNATURE:	
ADDRESS:		

SERVICES PROVIDED:	IDENTIFICATION:		ID NUMBER:
☐ JURAT	☐ ID CARD	☐ CREDIBLE WITNESS	
☐ OATH	☐ PASSPORT	☐ KNOWN PERSONALLY	ISSUED BY:
☐ ACKNOWLEDGEMENT	☐ DRIVERS LICENSE		DATE ISSUE : / EXPIRATION DATE:
☐ OTHER :	☐ OTHER :		

WITNESS FULL NAME:	EMAIL:
PHONE NUMBER:	WITNESS SIGNATURE:
ADDRESS:	

DOCUMENT TYPE:	DATE/TIME NOTARIZED:	DOCUMENT DATE:	FEE CHARGED:

COMMENTS:	RECORD NUMBER: 116

NOTARY RECORD

FULL NAME:

EMAIL:

THUMB PRINT

PHONE NUMBER:

SIGNER'S SIGNATURE:

ADDRESS:

SERVICES PROVIDED:
- [ ] JURAT
- [ ] OATH
- [ ] ACKNOWLEDGEMENT
- [ ] OTHER : ....

IDENTIFICATION:
- [ ] ID CARD
- [ ] PASSPORT
- [ ] DRIVERS LICENSE
- [ ] OTHER : ....
- [ ] CREDIBLE WITNESS
- [ ] KNOWN PERSONALLY

ID NUMBER:

ISSUED BY:

DATE ISSUE :

EXPIRATION DATE:

WITNESS FULL NAME:

EMAIL:

PHONE NUMBER:

WITNESS SIGNATURE:

ADDRESS:

DOCUMENT TYPE:

DATE/TIME NOTARIZED:

DOCUMENT DATE:

FEE CHARGED:

COMMENTS:

RECORD NUMBER: 117

NOTARY RECORD

FULL NAME:

EMAIL:

THUMB PRINT

PHONE NUMBER:

SIGNER'S SIGNATURE:

ADDRESS:

SERVICES PROVIDED:
- [ ] JURAT
- [ ] OATH
- [ ] ACKNOWLEDGEMENT
- [ ] OTHER : ....

IDENTIFICATION:
- [ ] ID CARD
- [ ] PASSPORT
- [ ] DRIVERS LICENSE
- [ ] OTHER : ....
- [ ] CREDIBLE WITNESS
- [ ] KNOWN PERSONALLY

ID NUMBER:

ISSUED BY:

DATE ISSUE :

EXPIRATION DATE:

WITNESS FULL NAME:

EMAIL:

PHONE NUMBER:

WITNESS SIGNATURE:

ADDRESS:

DOCUMENT TYPE:

DATE/TIME NOTARIZED:

DOCUMENT DATE:

FEE CHARGED:

COMMENTS:

RECORD NUMBER: 118

NOTARY RECORD

FULL NAME:	EMAIL:	THUMB PRINT
PHONE NUMBER:	SIGNER'S SIGNATURE:	
ADDRESS:		

SERVICES PROVIDED:	IDENTIFICATION:		ID NUMBER:
☐ JURAT	☐ ID CARD	☐ CREDIBLE WITNESS	
☐ OATH	☐ PASSPORT	☐ KNOWN PERSONALLY	ISSUED BY:
☐ ACKNOWLEDGEMENT	☐ DRIVERS LICENSE		DATE ISSUE : / EXPIRATION DATE:
☐ OTHER :	☐ OTHER :		

WITNESS FULL NAME:	EMAIL:
PHONE NUMBER:	WITNESS SIGNATURE:
ADDRESS:	

DOCUMENT TYPE:	DATE/TIME NOTARIZED:	DOCUMENT DATE:	FEE CHARGED:
COMMENTS:			RECORD NUMBER: **119**

NOTARY RECORD

FULL NAME:	EMAIL:	THUMB PRINT
PHONE NUMBER:	SIGNER'S SIGNATURE:	
ADDRESS:		

SERVICES PROVIDED:	IDENTIFICATION:		ID NUMBER:
☐ JURAT	☐ ID CARD	☐ CREDIBLE WITNESS	
☐ OATH	☐ PASSPORT	☐ KNOWN PERSONALLY	ISSUED BY:
☐ ACKNOWLEDGEMENT	☐ DRIVERS LICENSE		DATE ISSUE : / EXPIRATION DATE:
☐ OTHER :	☐ OTHER :		

WITNESS FULL NAME:	EMAIL:
PHONE NUMBER:	WITNESS SIGNATURE:
ADDRESS:	

DOCUMENT TYPE:	DATE/TIME NOTARIZED:	DOCUMENT DATE:	FEE CHARGED:
COMMENTS:			RECORD NUMBER: **120**

NOTARY RECORD

FULL NAME:

EMAIL:

THUMB PRINT

PHONE NUMBER:

SIGNER'S SIGNATURE:

ADDRESS:

SERVICES PROVIDED:
- ☐ JURAT
- ☐ OATH
- ☐ ACKNOWLEDGEMENT
- ☐ OTHER : ....

IDENTIFICATION:
- ☐ ID CARD
- ☐ PASSPORT
- ☐ DRIVERS LICENSE
- ☐ OTHER : ....

- ☐ CREDIBLE WITNESS
- ☐ KNOWN PERSONALLY

ID NUMBER:

ISSUED BY:

DATE ISSUE :

EXPIRATION DATE:

WITNESS FULL NAME:

EMAIL:

PHONE NUMBER:

WITNESS SIGNATURE:

ADDRESS:

DOCUMENT TYPE:	DATE/TIME NOTARIZED:	DOCUMENT DATE:	FEE CHARGED:

COMMENTS:

RECORD NUMBER: **121**

NOTARY RECORD

FULL NAME:

EMAIL:

THUMB PRINT

PHONE NUMBER:

SIGNER'S SIGNATURE:

ADDRESS:

SERVICES PROVIDED:
- ☐ JURAT
- ☐ OATH
- ☐ ACKNOWLEDGEMENT
- ☐ OTHER : ....

IDENTIFICATION:
- ☐ ID CARD
- ☐ PASSPORT
- ☐ DRIVERS LICENSE
- ☐ OTHER : ....

- ☐ CREDIBLE WITNESS
- ☐ KNOWN PERSONALLY

ID NUMBER:

ISSUED BY:

DATE ISSUE :

EXPIRATION DATE:

WITNESS FULL NAME:

EMAIL:

PHONE NUMBER:

WITNESS SIGNATURE:

ADDRESS:

DOCUMENT TYPE:	DATE/TIME NOTARIZED:	DOCUMENT DATE:	FEE CHARGED:

COMMENTS:

RECORD NUMBER: **122**

NOTARY RECORD

FULL NAME:	EMAIL:	THUMB PRINT
PHONE NUMBER:	SIGNER'S SIGNATURE:	
ADDRESS:		

SERVICES PROVIDED:
- ☐ JURAT
- ☐ OATH
- ☐ ACKNOWLEDGEMENT
- ☐ OTHER : ....

IDENTIFICATION:
- ☐ ID CARD
- ☐ PASSPORT
- ☐ DRIVERS LICENSE
- ☐ OTHER : ....

- ☐ CREDIBLE WITNESS
- ☐ KNOWN PERSONALLY

ID NUMBER:

ISSUED BY:

DATE ISSUE : EXPIRATION DATE:

WITNESS FULL NAME:	EMAIL:
PHONE NUMBER:	WITNESS SIGNATURE:
ADDRESS:	

DOCUMENT TYPE:	DATE/TIME NOTARIZED:	DOCUMENT DATE:	FEE CHARGED:

COMMENTS:	RECORD NUMBER: **123**

NOTARY RECORD

FULL NAME:	EMAIL:	THUMB PRINT
PHONE NUMBER:	SIGNER'S SIGNATURE:	
ADDRESS:		

SERVICES PROVIDED:
- ☐ JURAT
- ☐ OATH
- ☐ ACKNOWLEDGEMENT
- ☐ OTHER : ....

IDENTIFICATION:
- ☐ ID CARD
- ☐ PASSPORT
- ☐ DRIVERS LICENSE
- ☐ OTHER : ....

- ☐ CREDIBLE WITNESS
- ☐ KNOWN PERSONALLY

ID NUMBER:

ISSUED BY:

DATE ISSUE : EXPIRATION DATE:

WITNESS FULL NAME:	EMAIL:
PHONE NUMBER:	WITNESS SIGNATURE:
ADDRESS:	

DOCUMENT TYPE:	DATE/TIME NOTARIZED:	DOCUMENT DATE:	FEE CHARGED:

COMMENTS:	RECORD NUMBER: **124**

NOTARY RECORD

FULL NAME:

EMAIL:

THUMB PRINT

PHONE NUMBER:

SIGNER'S SIGNATURE:

ADDRESS:

SERVICES PROVIDED:
- ☐ JURAT
- ☐ OATH
- ☐ ACKNOWLEDGEMENT
- ☐ OTHER : ....

IDENTIFICATION:
- ☐ ID CARD
- ☐ PASSPORT
- ☐ DRIVERS LICENSE
- ☐ OTHER : ....

- ☐ CREDIBLE WITNESS
- ☐ KNOWN PERSONALLY

ID NUMBER:

ISSUED BY:

DATE ISSUE :

EXPIRATION DATE:

WITNESS FULL NAME:

EMAIL:

PHONE NUMBER:

WITNESS SIGNATURE:

ADDRESS:

DOCUMENT TYPE:

DATE/TIME NOTARIZED:

DOCUMENT DATE:

FEE CHARGED:

COMMENTS:

RECORD NUMBER: **125**

NOTARY RECORD

FULL NAME:

EMAIL:

THUMB PRINT

PHONE NUMBER:

SIGNER'S SIGNATURE:

ADDRESS:

SERVICES PROVIDED:
- ☐ JURAT
- ☐ OATH
- ☐ ACKNOWLEDGEMENT
- ☐ OTHER : ....

IDENTIFICATION:
- ☐ ID CARD
- ☐ PASSPORT
- ☐ DRIVERS LICENSE
- ☐ OTHER : ....

- ☐ CREDIBLE WITNESS
- ☐ KNOWN PERSONALLY

ID NUMBER:

ISSUED BY:

DATE ISSUE :

EXPIRATION DATE:

WITNESS FULL NAME:

EMAIL:

PHONE NUMBER:

WITNESS SIGNATURE:

ADDRESS:

DOCUMENT TYPE:

DATE/TIME NOTARIZED:

DOCUMENT DATE:

FEE CHARGED:

COMMENTS:

RECORD NUMBER: **126**

NOTARY RECORD

FULL NAME:	EMAIL:	THUMB PRINT
PHONE NUMBER:	SIGNER'S SIGNATURE:	
ADDRESS:		

SERVICES PROVIDED:	IDENTIFICATION:		ID NUMBER:
☐ JURAT	☐ ID CARD	☐ CREDIBLE WITNESS	
☐ OATH	☐ PASSPORT	☐ KNOWN PERSONALLY	ISSUED BY:
☐ ACKNOWLEDGEMENT	☐ DRIVERS LICENSE		DATE ISSUE :
☐ OTHER :	☐ OTHER :		EXPIRATION DATE:

WITNESS FULL NAME:	EMAIL:
PHONE NUMBER:	WITNESS SIGNATURE:
ADDRESS:	

DOCUMENT TYPE:	DATE/TIME NOTARIZED:	DOCUMENT DATE:	FEE CHARGED:
COMMENTS:		RECORD NUMBER:	**127**

NOTARY RECORD

FULL NAME:	EMAIL:	THUMB PRINT
PHONE NUMBER:	SIGNER'S SIGNATURE:	
ADDRESS:		

SERVICES PROVIDED:	IDENTIFICATION:		ID NUMBER:
☐ JURAT	☐ ID CARD	☐ CREDIBLE WITNESS	
☐ OATH	☐ PASSPORT	☐ KNOWN PERSONALLY	ISSUED BY:
☐ ACKNOWLEDGEMENT	☐ DRIVERS LICENSE		DATE ISSUE :
☐ OTHER :	☐ OTHER :		EXPIRATION DATE:

WITNESS FULL NAME:	EMAIL:
PHONE NUMBER:	WITNESS SIGNATURE:
ADDRESS:	

DOCUMENT TYPE:	DATE/TIME NOTARIZED:	DOCUMENT DATE:	FEE CHARGED:
COMMENTS:		RECORD NUMBER:	**128**

NOTARY RECORD

FULL NAME:

EMAIL:

THUMB PRINT

PHONE NUMBER:

SIGNER'S SIGNATURE:

ADDRESS:

SERVICES PROVIDED:
- ☐ JURAT
- ☐ OATH
- ☐ ACKNOWLEDGEMENT
- ☐ OTHER : ....

IDENTIFICATION:
- ☐ ID CARD
- ☐ PASSPORT
- ☐ DRIVERS LICENSE
- ☐ OTHER : ....

- ☐ CREDIBLE WITNESS
- ☐ KNOWN PERSONALLY

ID NUMBER:

ISSUED BY:

DATE ISSUE :

EXPIRATION DATE:

WITNESS FULL NAME:

EMAIL:

PHONE NUMBER:

WITNESS SIGNATURE:

ADDRESS:

DOCUMENT TYPE:	DATE/TIME NOTARIZED:	DOCUMENT DATE:	FEE CHARGED:

COMMENTS:

RECORD NUMBER: **129**

NOTARY RECORD

FULL NAME:

EMAIL:

THUMB PRINT

PHONE NUMBER:

SIGNER'S SIGNATURE:

ADDRESS:

SERVICES PROVIDED:
- ☐ JURAT
- ☐ OATH
- ☐ ACKNOWLEDGEMENT
- ☐ OTHER : ....

IDENTIFICATION:
- ☐ ID CARD
- ☐ PASSPORT
- ☐ DRIVERS LICENSE
- ☐ OTHER : ....

- ☐ CREDIBLE WITNESS
- ☐ KNOWN PERSONALLY

ID NUMBER:

ISSUED BY:

DATE ISSUE :

EXPIRATION DATE:

WITNESS FULL NAME:

EMAIL:

PHONE NUMBER:

WITNESS SIGNATURE:

ADDRESS:

DOCUMENT TYPE:	DATE/TIME NOTARIZED:	DOCUMENT DATE:	FEE CHARGED:

COMMENTS:

RECORD NUMBER: **130**

NOTARY RECORD

FULL NAME:	EMAIL:	THUMB PRINT
PHONE NUMBER:	SIGNER'S SIGNATURE:	
ADDRESS:		

SERVICES PROVIDED:	IDENTIFICATION:		ID NUMBER:
☐ JURAT	☐ ID CARD	☐ CREDIBLE WITNESS	
☐ OATH	☐ PASSPORT	☐ KNOWN PERSONALLY	ISSUED BY:
☐ ACKNOWLEDGEMENT	☐ DRIVERS LICENSE		DATE ISSUE : / EXPIRATION DATE:
☐ OTHER :	☐ OTHER :		

WITNESS FULL NAME:	EMAIL:
PHONE NUMBER:	WITNESS SIGNATURE:
ADDRESS:	

DOCUMENT TYPE:	DATE/TIME NOTARIZED:	DOCUMENT DATE:	FEE CHARGED:

COMMENTS:	RECORD NUMBER: 131

NOTARY RECORD

FULL NAME:	EMAIL:	THUMB PRINT
PHONE NUMBER:	SIGNER'S SIGNATURE:	
ADDRESS:		

SERVICES PROVIDED:	IDENTIFICATION:		ID NUMBER:
☐ JURAT	☐ ID CARD	☐ CREDIBLE WITNESS	
☐ OATH	☐ PASSPORT	☐ KNOWN PERSONALLY	ISSUED BY:
☐ ACKNOWLEDGEMENT	☐ DRIVERS LICENSE		DATE ISSUE : / EXPIRATION DATE:
☐ OTHER :	☐ OTHER :		

WITNESS FULL NAME:	EMAIL:
PHONE NUMBER:	WITNESS SIGNATURE:
ADDRESS:	

DOCUMENT TYPE:	DATE/TIME NOTARIZED:	DOCUMENT DATE:	FEE CHARGED:

COMMENTS:	RECORD NUMBER: 132

NOTARY RECORD

FULL NAME:	EMAIL:	THUMB PRINT
PHONE NUMBER:	SIGNER'S SIGNATURE:	
ADDRESS:		

SERVICES PROVIDED:	IDENTIFICATION:		ID NUMBER:
☐ JURAT	☐ ID CARD	☐ CREDIBLE WITNESS	
☐ OATH	☐ PASSPORT	☐ KNOWN PERSONALLY	ISSUED BY:
☐ ACKNOWLEDGEMENT	☐ DRIVERS LICENSE		DATE ISSUE : / EXPIRATION DATE:
☐ OTHER :	☐ OTHER :		

WITNESS FULL NAME:	EMAIL:
PHONE NUMBER:	WITNESS SIGNATURE:
ADDRESS:	

DOCUMENT TYPE:	DATE/TIME NOTARIZED:	DOCUMENT DATE:	FEE CHARGED:

COMMENTS:	RECORD NUMBER: **133**

NOTARY RECORD

FULL NAME:	EMAIL:	THUMB PRINT
PHONE NUMBER:	SIGNER'S SIGNATURE:	
ADDRESS:		

SERVICES PROVIDED:	IDENTIFICATION:		ID NUMBER:
☐ JURAT	☐ ID CARD	☐ CREDIBLE WITNESS	
☐ OATH	☐ PASSPORT	☐ KNOWN PERSONALLY	ISSUED BY:
☐ ACKNOWLEDGEMENT	☐ DRIVERS LICENSE		DATE ISSUE : / EXPIRATION DATE:
☐ OTHER :	☐ OTHER :		

WITNESS FULL NAME:	EMAIL:
PHONE NUMBER:	WITNESS SIGNATURE:
ADDRESS:	

DOCUMENT TYPE:	DATE/TIME NOTARIZED:	DOCUMENT DATE:	FEE CHARGED:

COMMENTS:	RECORD NUMBER: **134**

NOTARY RECORD

FULL NAME:	EMAIL:	THUMB PRINT
PHONE NUMBER:	SIGNER'S SIGNATURE:	
ADDRESS:		

SERVICES PROVIDED:	IDENTIFICATION:		ID NUMBER:
☐ JURAT	☐ ID CARD	☐ CREDIBLE WITNESS	
☐ OATH	☐ PASSPORT	☐ KNOWN PERSONALLY	ISSUED BY:
☐ ACKNOWLEDGEMENT	☐ DRIVERS LICENSE		DATE ISSUE : / EXPIRATION DATE:
☐ OTHER :	☐ OTHER :		

WITNESS FULL NAME:	EMAIL:
PHONE NUMBER:	WITNESS SIGNATURE:
ADDRESS:	

DOCUMENT TYPE:	DATE/TIME NOTARIZED:	DOCUMENT DATE:	FEE CHARGED:

COMMENTS:	RECORD NUMBER: **135**

NOTARY RECORD

FULL NAME:	EMAIL:	THUMB PRINT
PHONE NUMBER:	SIGNER'S SIGNATURE:	
ADDRESS:		

SERVICES PROVIDED:	IDENTIFICATION:		ID NUMBER:
☐ JURAT	☐ ID CARD	☐ CREDIBLE WITNESS	
☐ OATH	☐ PASSPORT	☐ KNOWN PERSONALLY	ISSUED BY:
☐ ACKNOWLEDGEMENT	☐ DRIVERS LICENSE		DATE ISSUE : / EXPIRATION DATE:
☐ OTHER :	☐ OTHER :		

WITNESS FULL NAME:	EMAIL:
PHONE NUMBER:	WITNESS SIGNATURE:
ADDRESS:	

DOCUMENT TYPE:	DATE/TIME NOTARIZED:	DOCUMENT DATE:	FEE CHARGED:

COMMENTS:	RECORD NUMBER: **136**

NOTARY RECORD

FULL NAME:	EMAIL:	THUMB PRINT
PHONE NUMBER:	SIGNER'S SIGNATURE:	
ADDRESS:		

SERVICES PROVIDED:	IDENTIFICATION:		ID NUMBER:
☐ JURAT	☐ ID CARD	☐ CREDIBLE WITNESS	
☐ OATH	☐ PASSPORT	☐ KNOWN PERSONALLY	ISSUED BY:
☐ ACKNOWLEDGEMENT	☐ DRIVERS LICENSE		DATE ISSUE : EXPIRATION DATE:
☐ OTHER :	☐ OTHER :		

WITNESS FULL NAME:	EMAIL:
PHONE NUMBER:	WITNESS SIGNATURE:
ADDRESS:	

DOCUMENT TYPE:	DATE/TIME NOTARIZED:	DOCUMENT DATE:	FEE CHARGED:

COMMENTS:	RECORD NUMBER: 137

NOTARY RECORD

FULL NAME:	EMAIL:	THUMB PRINT
PHONE NUMBER:	SIGNER'S SIGNATURE:	
ADDRESS:		

SERVICES PROVIDED:	IDENTIFICATION:		ID NUMBER:
☐ JURAT	☐ ID CARD	☐ CREDIBLE WITNESS	
☐ OATH	☐ PASSPORT	☐ KNOWN PERSONALLY	ISSUED BY:
☐ ACKNOWLEDGEMENT	☐ DRIVERS LICENSE		DATE ISSUE : EXPIRATION DATE:
☐ OTHER :	☐ OTHER :		

WITNESS FULL NAME:	EMAIL:
PHONE NUMBER:	WITNESS SIGNATURE:
ADDRESS:	

DOCUMENT TYPE:	DATE/TIME NOTARIZED:	DOCUMENT DATE:	FEE CHARGED:

COMMENTS:	RECORD NUMBER: 138

NOTARY RECORD

FULL NAME:	EMAIL:	THUMB PRINT
PHONE NUMBER:	SIGNER'S SIGNATURE:	
ADDRESS:		

SERVICES PROVIDED:
- ☐ JURAT
- ☐ OATH
- ☐ ACKNOWLEDGEMENT
- ☐ OTHER : ....

IDENTIFICATION:
- ☐ ID CARD
- ☐ PASSPORT
- ☐ DRIVERS LICENSE
- ☐ OTHER : ....

- ☐ CREDIBLE WITNESS
- ☐ KNOWN PERSONALLY

ID NUMBER:

ISSUED BY:

DATE ISSUE :

EXPIRATION DATE:

WITNESS FULL NAME:	EMAIL:
PHONE NUMBER:	WITNESS SIGNATURE:
ADDRESS:	

DOCUMENT TYPE:	DATE/TIME NOTARIZED:	DOCUMENT DATE:	FEE CHARGED:

COMMENTS:	RECORD NUMBER: **139**

NOTARY RECORD

FULL NAME:	EMAIL:	THUMB PRINT
PHONE NUMBER:	SIGNER'S SIGNATURE:	
ADDRESS:		

SERVICES PROVIDED:
- ☐ JURAT
- ☐ OATH
- ☐ ACKNOWLEDGEMENT
- ☐ OTHER : ....

IDENTIFICATION:
- ☐ ID CARD
- ☐ PASSPORT
- ☐ DRIVERS LICENSE
- ☐ OTHER : ....

- ☐ CREDIBLE WITNESS
- ☐ KNOWN PERSONALLY

ID NUMBER:

ISSUED BY:

DATE ISSUE :

EXPIRATION DATE:

WITNESS FULL NAME:	EMAIL:
PHONE NUMBER:	WITNESS SIGNATURE:
ADDRESS:	

DOCUMENT TYPE:	DATE/TIME NOTARIZED:	DOCUMENT DATE:	FEE CHARGED:

COMMENTS:	RECORD NUMBER: **140**

NOTARY RECORD

FULL NAME:

EMAIL:

THUMB PRINT

PHONE NUMBER:

SIGNER'S SIGNATURE:

ADDRESS:

SERVICES PROVIDED:	IDENTIFICATION:		ID NUMBER:
☐ JURAT	☐ ID CARD	☐ CREDIBLE WITNESS	
☐ OATH	☐ PASSPORT	☐ KNOWN PERSONALLY	**ISSUED BY:**
☐ ACKNOWLEDGEMENT	☐ DRIVERS LICENSE		**DATE ISSUE :** / **EXPIRATION DATE:**
☐ OTHER :	☐ OTHER :		

WITNESS FULL NAME:

EMAIL:

PHONE NUMBER:

WITNESS SIGNATURE:

ADDRESS:

DOCUMENT TYPE:	DATE/TIME NOTARIZED:	DOCUMENT DATE:	FEE CHARGED:

COMMENTS:	RECORD NUMBER: **141**

NOTARY RECORD

FULL NAME:

EMAIL:

THUMB PRINT

PHONE NUMBER:

SIGNER'S SIGNATURE:

ADDRESS:

SERVICES PROVIDED:	IDENTIFICATION:		ID NUMBER:
☐ JURAT	☐ ID CARD	☐ CREDIBLE WITNESS	
☐ OATH	☐ PASSPORT	☐ KNOWN PERSONALLY	**ISSUED BY:**
☐ ACKNOWLEDGEMENT	☐ DRIVERS LICENSE		**DATE ISSUE :** / **EXPIRATION DATE:**
☐ OTHER :	☐ OTHER :		

WITNESS FULL NAME:

EMAIL:

PHONE NUMBER:

WITNESS SIGNATURE:

ADDRESS:

DOCUMENT TYPE:	DATE/TIME NOTARIZED:	DOCUMENT DATE:	FEE CHARGED:

COMMENTS:	RECORD NUMBER: **142**

NOTARY RECORD

FULL NAME:	EMAIL:	THUMB PRINT
PHONE NUMBER:	SIGNER'S SIGNATURE:	
ADDRESS:		

SERVICES PROVIDED:	IDENTIFICATION:		ID NUMBER:
☐ JURAT	☐ ID CARD	☐ CREDIBLE WITNESS	
☐ OATH	☐ PASSPORT	☐ KNOWN PERSONALLY	ISSUED BY:
☐ ACKNOWLEDGEMENT	☐ DRIVERS LICENSE		DATE ISSUE : / EXPIRATION DATE:
☐ OTHER :	☐ OTHER :		

WITNESS FULL NAME:	EMAIL:
PHONE NUMBER:	WITNESS SIGNATURE:
ADDRESS:	

DOCUMENT TYPE:	DATE/TIME NOTARIZED:	DOCUMENT DATE:	FEE CHARGED:

COMMENTS:	RECORD NUMBER: **143**

NOTARY RECORD

FULL NAME:	EMAIL:	THUMB PRINT
PHONE NUMBER:	SIGNER'S SIGNATURE:	
ADDRESS:		

SERVICES PROVIDED:	IDENTIFICATION:		ID NUMBER:
☐ JURAT	☐ ID CARD	☐ CREDIBLE WITNESS	
☐ OATH	☐ PASSPORT	☐ KNOWN PERSONALLY	ISSUED BY:
☐ ACKNOWLEDGEMENT	☐ DRIVERS LICENSE		DATE ISSUE : / EXPIRATION DATE:
☐ OTHER :	☐ OTHER :		

WITNESS FULL NAME:	EMAIL:
PHONE NUMBER:	WITNESS SIGNATURE:
ADDRESS:	

DOCUMENT TYPE:	DATE/TIME NOTARIZED:	DOCUMENT DATE:	FEE CHARGED:

COMMENTS:	RECORD NUMBER: **144**

NOTARY RECORD

FULL NAME:

EMAIL:

THUMB PRINT

PHONE NUMBER:

SIGNER'S SIGNATURE:

ADDRESS:

SERVICES PROVIDED:
- ☐ JURAT
- ☐ OATH
- ☐ ACKNOWLEDGEMENT
- ☐ OTHER : ....

IDENTIFICATION:
- ☐ ID CARD
- ☐ PASSPORT
- ☐ DRIVERS LICENSE
- ☐ OTHER : ....

- ☐ CREDIBLE WITNESS
- ☐ KNOWN PERSONALLY

ID NUMBER:

ISSUED BY:

DATE ISSUE :

EXPIRATION DATE:

WITNESS FULL NAME:

EMAIL:

PHONE NUMBER:

WITNESS SIGNATURE:

ADDRESS:

DOCUMENT TYPE:	DATE/TIME NOTARIZED:	DOCUMENT DATE:	FEE CHARGED:

COMMENTS:

RECORD NUMBER: **145**

NOTARY RECORD

FULL NAME:

EMAIL:

THUMB PRINT

PHONE NUMBER:

SIGNER'S SIGNATURE:

ADDRESS:

SERVICES PROVIDED:
- ☐ JURAT
- ☐ OATH
- ☐ ACKNOWLEDGEMENT
- ☐ OTHER : ....

IDENTIFICATION:
- ☐ ID CARD
- ☐ PASSPORT
- ☐ DRIVERS LICENSE
- ☐ OTHER : ....

- ☐ CREDIBLE WITNESS
- ☐ KNOWN PERSONALLY

ID NUMBER:

ISSUED BY:

DATE ISSUE :

EXPIRATION DATE:

WITNESS FULL NAME:

EMAIL:

PHONE NUMBER:

WITNESS SIGNATURE:

ADDRESS:

DOCUMENT TYPE:	DATE/TIME NOTARIZED:	DOCUMENT DATE:	FEE CHARGED:

COMMENTS:

RECORD NUMBER: **146**

NOTARY RECORD

FULL NAME:	EMAIL:	THUMB PRINT
PHONE NUMBER:	SIGNER'S SIGNATURE:	
ADDRESS:		

SERVICES PROVIDED:	IDENTIFICATION:		ID NUMBER:
☐ JURAT	☐ ID CARD	☐ CREDIBLE WITNESS	
☐ OATH	☐ PASSPORT	☐ KNOWN PERSONALLY	ISSUED BY:
☐ ACKNOWLEDGEMENT	☐ DRIVERS LICENSE		DATE ISSUE : / EXPIRATION DATE:
☐ OTHER :	☐ OTHER :		

WITNESS FULL NAME:	EMAIL:
PHONE NUMBER:	WITNESS SIGNATURE:
ADDRESS:	

DOCUMENT TYPE:	DATE/TIME NOTARIZED:	DOCUMENT DATE:	FEE CHARGED:
COMMENTS:		RECORD NUMBER:	**147**

NOTARY RECORD

FULL NAME:	EMAIL:	THUMB PRINT
PHONE NUMBER:	SIGNER'S SIGNATURE:	
ADDRESS:		

SERVICES PROVIDED:	IDENTIFICATION:		ID NUMBER:
☐ JURAT	☐ ID CARD	☐ CREDIBLE WITNESS	
☐ OATH	☐ PASSPORT	☐ KNOWN PERSONALLY	ISSUED BY:
☐ ACKNOWLEDGEMENT	☐ DRIVERS LICENSE		DATE ISSUE : / EXPIRATION DATE:
☐ OTHER :	☐ OTHER :		

WITNESS FULL NAME:	EMAIL:
PHONE NUMBER:	WITNESS SIGNATURE:
ADDRESS:	

DOCUMENT TYPE:	DATE/TIME NOTARIZED:	DOCUMENT DATE:	FEE CHARGED:
COMMENTS:		RECORD NUMBER:	**148**

NOTARY RECORD

FULL NAME:

EMAIL:

THUMB PRINT

PHONE NUMBER:

SIGNER'S SIGNATURE:

ADDRESS:

SERVICES PROVIDED:	IDENTIFICATION:		ID NUMBER:
☐ JURAT	☐ ID CARD	☐ CREDIBLE WITNESS	
☐ OATH	☐ PASSPORT	☐ KNOWN PERSONALLY	ISSUED BY:
☐ ACKNOWLEDGEMENT	☐ DRIVERS LICENSE		DATE ISSUE :
☐ OTHER :	☐ OTHER :		EXPIRATION DATE:

WITNESS FULL NAME:

EMAIL:

PHONE NUMBER:

WITNESS SIGNATURE:

ADDRESS:

DOCUMENT TYPE:	DATE/TIME NOTARIZED:	DOCUMENT DATE:	FEE CHARGED:

COMMENTS:

RECORD NUMBER: **149**

NOTARY RECORD

FULL NAME:

EMAIL:

THUMB PRINT

PHONE NUMBER:

SIGNER'S SIGNATURE:

ADDRESS:

SERVICES PROVIDED:	IDENTIFICATION:		ID NUMBER:
☐ JURAT	☐ ID CARD	☐ CREDIBLE WITNESS	
☐ OATH	☐ PASSPORT	☐ KNOWN PERSONALLY	ISSUED BY:
☐ ACKNOWLEDGEMENT	☐ DRIVERS LICENSE		DATE ISSUE :
☐ OTHER :	☐ OTHER :		EXPIRATION DATE:

WITNESS FULL NAME:

EMAIL:

PHONE NUMBER:

WITNESS SIGNATURE:

ADDRESS:

DOCUMENT TYPE:	DATE/TIME NOTARIZED:	DOCUMENT DATE:	FEE CHARGED:

COMMENTS:

RECORD NUMBER: **150**

NOTARY RECORD

FULL NAME:	EMAIL:	THUMB PRINT
PHONE NUMBER:	SIGNER'S SIGNATURE:	
ADDRESS:		

SERVICES PROVIDED:	IDENTIFICATION:		ID NUMBER:
☐ JURAT	☐ ID CARD	☐ CREDIBLE WITNESS	
☐ OATH	☐ PASSPORT	☐ KNOWN PERSONALLY	ISSUED BY:
☐ ACKNOWLEDGEMENT	☐ DRIVERS LICENSE		DATE ISSUE : / EXPIRATION DATE:
☐ OTHER :	☐ OTHER :		

WITNESS FULL NAME:	EMAIL:
PHONE NUMBER:	WITNESS SIGNATURE:
ADDRESS:	

DOCUMENT TYPE:	DATE/TIME NOTARIZED:	DOCUMENT DATE:	FEE CHARGED:
COMMENTS:			RECORD NUMBER: **151**

NOTARY RECORD

FULL NAME:	EMAIL:	THUMB PRINT
PHONE NUMBER:	SIGNER'S SIGNATURE:	
ADDRESS:		

SERVICES PROVIDED:	IDENTIFICATION:		ID NUMBER:
☐ JURAT	☐ ID CARD	☐ CREDIBLE WITNESS	
☐ OATH	☐ PASSPORT	☐ KNOWN PERSONALLY	ISSUED BY:
☐ ACKNOWLEDGEMENT	☐ DRIVERS LICENSE		DATE ISSUE : / EXPIRATION DATE:
☐ OTHER :	☐ OTHER :		

WITNESS FULL NAME:	EMAIL:
PHONE NUMBER:	WITNESS SIGNATURE:
ADDRESS:	

DOCUMENT TYPE:	DATE/TIME NOTARIZED:	DOCUMENT DATE:	FEE CHARGED:
COMMENTS:			RECORD NUMBER: **152**

NOTARY RECORD

FULL NAME:	EMAIL:	THUMB PRINT
PHONE NUMBER:	SIGNER'S SIGNATURE:	
ADDRESS:		

SERVICES PROVIDED:	IDENTIFICATION:		ID NUMBER:
☐ JURAT	☐ ID CARD	☐ CREDIBLE WITNESS	
☐ OATH	☐ PASSPORT	☐ KNOWN PERSONALLY	ISSUED BY:
☐ ACKNOWLEDGEMENT	☐ DRIVERS LICENSE		DATE ISSUE : / EXPIRATION DATE:
☐ OTHER :	☐ OTHER :		

WITNESS FULL NAME:	EMAIL:
PHONE NUMBER:	WITNESS SIGNATURE:
ADDRESS:	

DOCUMENT TYPE:	DATE/TIME NOTARIZED:	DOCUMENT DATE:	FEE CHARGED:

COMMENTS:	RECORD NUMBER: **153**

NOTARY RECORD

FULL NAME:	EMAIL:	THUMB PRINT
PHONE NUMBER:	SIGNER'S SIGNATURE:	
ADDRESS:		

SERVICES PROVIDED:	IDENTIFICATION:		ID NUMBER:
☐ JURAT	☐ ID CARD	☐ CREDIBLE WITNESS	
☐ OATH	☐ PASSPORT	☐ KNOWN PERSONALLY	ISSUED BY:
☐ ACKNOWLEDGEMENT	☐ DRIVERS LICENSE		DATE ISSUE : / EXPIRATION DATE:
☐ OTHER :	☐ OTHER :		

WITNESS FULL NAME:	EMAIL:
PHONE NUMBER:	WITNESS SIGNATURE:
ADDRESS:	

DOCUMENT TYPE:	DATE/TIME NOTARIZED:	DOCUMENT DATE:	FEE CHARGED:

COMMENTS:	RECORD NUMBER: **154**

NOTARY RECORD

FULL NAME:	EMAIL:	THUMB PRINT
PHONE NUMBER:	SIGNER'S SIGNATURE:	
ADDRESS:		

SERVICES PROVIDED:	IDENTIFICATION:		ID NUMBER:	
☐ JURAT	☐ ID CARD	☐ CREDIBLE WITNESS		
☐ OATH	☐ PASSPORT	☐ KNOWN PERSONALLY	ISSUED BY:	
☐ ACKNOWLEDGEMENT	☐ DRIVERS LICENSE		DATE ISSUE :	EXPIRATION DATE:
☐ OTHER :	☐ OTHER :			

WITNESS FULL NAME:	EMAIL:
PHONE NUMBER:	WITNESS SIGNATURE:
ADDRESS:	

DOCUMENT TYPE:	DATE/TIME NOTARIZED:	DOCUMENT DATE:	FEE CHARGED:

COMMENTS:	RECORD NUMBER: 155

NOTARY RECORD

FULL NAME:	EMAIL:	THUMB PRINT
PHONE NUMBER:	SIGNER'S SIGNATURE:	
ADDRESS:		

SERVICES PROVIDED:	IDENTIFICATION:		ID NUMBER:	
☐ JURAT	☐ ID CARD	☐ CREDIBLE WITNESS		
☐ OATH	☐ PASSPORT	☐ KNOWN PERSONALLY	ISSUED BY:	
☐ ACKNOWLEDGEMENT	☐ DRIVERS LICENSE		DATE ISSUE :	EXPIRATION DATE:
☐ OTHER :	☐ OTHER :			

WITNESS FULL NAME:	EMAIL:
PHONE NUMBER:	WITNESS SIGNATURE:
ADDRESS:	

DOCUMENT TYPE:	DATE/TIME NOTARIZED:	DOCUMENT DATE:	FEE CHARGED:

COMMENTS:	RECORD NUMBER: 156

NOTARY RECORD

FULL NAME:

EMAIL:

THUMB PRINT

PHONE NUMBER:

SIGNER'S SIGNATURE:

ADDRESS:

SERVICES PROVIDED:
- ☐ JURAT
- ☐ OATH
- ☐ ACKNOWLEDGEMENT
- ☐ OTHER : ....

IDENTIFICATION:
- ☐ ID CARD
- ☐ PASSPORT
- ☐ DRIVERS LICENSE
- ☐ OTHER : ....

- ☐ CREDIBLE WITNESS
- ☐ KNOWN PERSONALLY

ID NUMBER:

ISSUED BY:

DATE ISSUE :

EXPIRATION DATE:

WITNESS FULL NAME:

EMAIL:

PHONE NUMBER:

WITNESS SIGNATURE:

ADDRESS:

DOCUMENT TYPE:	DATE/TIME NOTARIZED:	DOCUMENT DATE:	FEE CHARGED:

COMMENTS:

RECORD NUMBER: **157**

NOTARY RECORD

FULL NAME:

EMAIL:

THUMB PRINT

PHONE NUMBER:

SIGNER'S SIGNATURE:

ADDRESS:

SERVICES PROVIDED:
- ☐ JURAT
- ☐ OATH
- ☐ ACKNOWLEDGEMENT
- ☐ OTHER : ....

IDENTIFICATION:
- ☐ ID CARD
- ☐ PASSPORT
- ☐ DRIVERS LICENSE
- ☐ OTHER : ....

- ☐ CREDIBLE WITNESS
- ☐ KNOWN PERSONALLY

ID NUMBER:

ISSUED BY:

DATE ISSUE :

EXPIRATION DATE:

WITNESS FULL NAME:

EMAIL:

PHONE NUMBER:

WITNESS SIGNATURE:

ADDRESS:

DOCUMENT TYPE:	DATE/TIME NOTARIZED:	DOCUMENT DATE:	FEE CHARGED:

COMMENTS:

RECORD NUMBER: **158**

NOTARY RECORD

FULL NAME:	EMAIL:	THUMB PRINT
PHONE NUMBER:	SIGNER'S SIGNATURE:	
ADDRESS:		

SERVICES PROVIDED:	IDENTIFICATION:		ID NUMBER:
☐ JURAT	☐ ID CARD	☐ CREDIBLE WITNESS	
☐ OATH	☐ PASSPORT	☐ KNOWN PERSONALLY	ISSUED BY:
☐ ACKNOWLEDGEMENT	☐ DRIVERS LICENSE		DATE ISSUE : / EXPIRATION DATE:
☐ OTHER :	☐ OTHER :		

WITNESS FULL NAME:	EMAIL:
PHONE NUMBER:	WITNESS SIGNATURE:
ADDRESS:	

DOCUMENT TYPE:	DATE/TIME NOTARIZED:	DOCUMENT DATE:	FEE CHARGED:
COMMENTS:			RECORD NUMBER: **159**

NOTARY RECORD

FULL NAME:	EMAIL:	THUMB PRINT
PHONE NUMBER:	SIGNER'S SIGNATURE:	
ADDRESS:		

SERVICES PROVIDED:	IDENTIFICATION:		ID NUMBER:
☐ JURAT	☐ ID CARD	☐ CREDIBLE WITNESS	
☐ OATH	☐ PASSPORT	☐ KNOWN PERSONALLY	ISSUED BY:
☐ ACKNOWLEDGEMENT	☐ DRIVERS LICENSE		DATE ISSUE : / EXPIRATION DATE:
☐ OTHER :	☐ OTHER :		

WITNESS FULL NAME:	EMAIL:
PHONE NUMBER:	WITNESS SIGNATURE:
ADDRESS:	

DOCUMENT TYPE:	DATE/TIME NOTARIZED:	DOCUMENT DATE:	FEE CHARGED:
COMMENTS:			RECORD NUMBER: **160**

NOTARY RECORD

FULL NAME:

EMAIL:

THUMB PRINT

PHONE NUMBER:

SIGNER'S SIGNATURE:

ADDRESS:

SERVICES PROVIDED:	IDENTIFICATION:		ID NUMBER:
☐ JURAT	☐ ID CARD	☐ CREDIBLE WITNESS	
☐ OATH	☐ PASSPORT	☐ KNOWN PERSONALLY	ISSUED BY:
☐ ACKNOWLEDGEMENT	☐ DRIVERS LICENSE		DATE ISSUE : / EXPIRATION DATE:
☐ OTHER :	☐ OTHER :		

WITNESS FULL NAME:

EMAIL:

PHONE NUMBER:

WITNESS SIGNATURE:

ADDRESS:

DOCUMENT TYPE:	DATE/TIME NOTARIZED:	DOCUMENT DATE:	FEE CHARGED:

COMMENTS:

RECORD NUMBER: **161**

NOTARY RECORD

FULL NAME:

EMAIL:

THUMB PRINT

PHONE NUMBER:

SIGNER'S SIGNATURE:

ADDRESS:

SERVICES PROVIDED:	IDENTIFICATION:		ID NUMBER:
☐ JURAT	☐ ID CARD	☐ CREDIBLE WITNESS	
☐ OATH	☐ PASSPORT	☐ KNOWN PERSONALLY	ISSUED BY:
☐ ACKNOWLEDGEMENT	☐ DRIVERS LICENSE		DATE ISSUE : / EXPIRATION DATE:
☐ OTHER :	☐ OTHER :		

WITNESS FULL NAME:

EMAIL:

PHONE NUMBER:

WITNESS SIGNATURE:

ADDRESS:

DOCUMENT TYPE:	DATE/TIME NOTARIZED:	DOCUMENT DATE:	FEE CHARGED:

COMMENTS:

RECORD NUMBER: **162**

NOTARY RECORD

FULL NAME:	EMAIL:	THUMB PRINT
PHONE NUMBER:	SIGNER'S SIGNATURE:	
ADDRESS:		

SERVICES PROVIDED:	IDENTIFICATION:		ID NUMBER:
☐ JURAT	☐ ID CARD	☐ CREDIBLE WITNESS	
☐ OATH	☐ PASSPORT	☐ KNOWN PERSONALLY	ISSUED BY:
☐ ACKNOWLEDGEMENT	☐ DRIVERS LICENSE		DATE ISSUE : / EXPIRATION DATE:
☐ OTHER :	☐ OTHER :		

WITNESS FULL NAME:	EMAIL:
PHONE NUMBER:	WITNESS SIGNATURE:
ADDRESS:	

DOCUMENT TYPE:	DATE/TIME NOTARIZED:	DOCUMENT DATE:	FEE CHARGED:
COMMENTS:		RECORD NUMBER:	**163**

NOTARY RECORD

FULL NAME:	EMAIL:	THUMB PRINT
PHONE NUMBER:	SIGNER'S SIGNATURE:	
ADDRESS:		

SERVICES PROVIDED:	IDENTIFICATION:		ID NUMBER:
☐ JURAT	☐ ID CARD	☐ CREDIBLE WITNESS	
☐ OATH	☐ PASSPORT	☐ KNOWN PERSONALLY	ISSUED BY:
☐ ACKNOWLEDGEMENT	☐ DRIVERS LICENSE		DATE ISSUE : / EXPIRATION DATE:
☐ OTHER :	☐ OTHER :		

WITNESS FULL NAME:	EMAIL:
PHONE NUMBER:	WITNESS SIGNATURE:
ADDRESS:	

DOCUMENT TYPE:	DATE/TIME NOTARIZED:	DOCUMENT DATE:	FEE CHARGED:
COMMENTS:		RECORD NUMBER:	**164**

NOTARY RECORD

FULL NAME:	EMAIL:	THUMB PRINT
PHONE NUMBER:	SIGNER'S SIGNATURE:	
ADDRESS:		

SERVICES PROVIDED:	IDENTIFICATION:		ID NUMBER:
☐ JURAT	☐ ID CARD	☐ CREDIBLE WITNESS	
☐ OATH	☐ PASSPORT	☐ KNOWN PERSONALLY	ISSUED BY:
☐ ACKNOWLEDGEMENT	☐ DRIVERS LICENSE		DATE ISSUE : / EXPIRATION DATE:
☐ OTHER :	☐ OTHER :		

WITNESS FULL NAME:	EMAIL:
PHONE NUMBER:	WITNESS SIGNATURE:
ADDRESS:	

DOCUMENT TYPE:	DATE/TIME NOTARIZED:	DOCUMENT DATE:	FEE CHARGED:

COMMENTS:	RECORD NUMBER: **165**

NOTARY RECORD

FULL NAME:	EMAIL:	THUMB PRINT
PHONE NUMBER:	SIGNER'S SIGNATURE:	
ADDRESS:		

SERVICES PROVIDED:	IDENTIFICATION:		ID NUMBER:
☐ JURAT	☐ ID CARD	☐ CREDIBLE WITNESS	
☐ OATH	☐ PASSPORT	☐ KNOWN PERSONALLY	ISSUED BY:
☐ ACKNOWLEDGEMENT	☐ DRIVERS LICENSE		DATE ISSUE : / EXPIRATION DATE:
☐ OTHER :	☐ OTHER :		

WITNESS FULL NAME:	EMAIL:
PHONE NUMBER:	WITNESS SIGNATURE:
ADDRESS:	

DOCUMENT TYPE:	DATE/TIME NOTARIZED:	DOCUMENT DATE:	FEE CHARGED:

COMMENTS:	RECORD NUMBER: **166**

NOTARY RECORD

FULL NAME:

EMAIL:

THUMB PRINT

PHONE NUMBER:

SIGNER'S SIGNATURE:

ADDRESS:

SERVICES PROVIDED:	IDENTIFICATION:		ID NUMBER:
☐ JURAT	☐ ID CARD	☐ CREDIBLE WITNESS	
☐ OATH	☐ PASSPORT	☐ KNOWN PERSONALLY	ISSUED BY:
☐ ACKNOWLEDGEMENT	☐ DRIVERS LICENSE		DATE ISSUE : / EXPIRATION DATE:
☐ OTHER :	☐ OTHER :		

WITNESS FULL NAME:

EMAIL:

PHONE NUMBER:

WITNESS SIGNATURE:

ADDRESS:

DOCUMENT TYPE:	DATE/TIME NOTARIZED:	DOCUMENT DATE:	FEE CHARGED:
COMMENTS:			RECORD NUMBER: **167**

NOTARY RECORD

FULL NAME:

EMAIL:

THUMB PRINT

PHONE NUMBER:

SIGNER'S SIGNATURE:

ADDRESS:

SERVICES PROVIDED:	IDENTIFICATION:		ID NUMBER:
☐ JURAT	☐ ID CARD	☐ CREDIBLE WITNESS	
☐ OATH	☐ PASSPORT	☐ KNOWN PERSONALLY	ISSUED BY:
☐ ACKNOWLEDGEMENT	☐ DRIVERS LICENSE		DATE ISSUE : / EXPIRATION DATE:
☐ OTHER :	☐ OTHER :		

WITNESS FULL NAME:

EMAIL:

PHONE NUMBER:

WITNESS SIGNATURE:

ADDRESS:

DOCUMENT TYPE:	DATE/TIME NOTARIZED:	DOCUMENT DATE:	FEE CHARGED:
COMMENTS:			RECORD NUMBER: **168**

NOTARY RECORD

FULL NAME:

EMAIL:

THUMB PRINT

PHONE NUMBER:

SIGNER'S SIGNATURE:

ADDRESS:

SERVICES PROVIDED:
- ☐ JURAT
- ☐ OATH
- ☐ ACKNOWLEDGEMENT
- ☐ OTHER : ....

IDENTIFICATION:
- ☐ ID CARD
- ☐ PASSPORT
- ☐ DRIVERS LICENSE
- ☐ OTHER : ....
- ☐ CREDIBLE WITNESS
- ☐ KNOWN PERSONALLY

ID NUMBER:

ISSUED BY:

DATE ISSUE :

EXPIRATION DATE:

WITNESS FULL NAME:

EMAIL:

PHONE NUMBER:

WITNESS SIGNATURE:

ADDRESS:

DOCUMENT TYPE:	DATE/TIME NOTARIZED:	DOCUMENT DATE:	FEE CHARGED:

COMMENTS:

RECORD NUMBER: **169**

NOTARY RECORD

FULL NAME:

EMAIL:

THUMB PRINT

PHONE NUMBER:

SIGNER'S SIGNATURE:

ADDRESS:

SERVICES PROVIDED:
- ☐ JURAT
- ☐ OATH
- ☐ ACKNOWLEDGEMENT
- ☐ OTHER : ....

IDENTIFICATION:
- ☐ ID CARD
- ☐ PASSPORT
- ☐ DRIVERS LICENSE
- ☐ OTHER : ....
- ☐ CREDIBLE WITNESS
- ☐ KNOWN PERSONALLY

ID NUMBER:

ISSUED BY:

DATE ISSUE :

EXPIRATION DATE:

WITNESS FULL NAME:

EMAIL:

PHONE NUMBER:

WITNESS SIGNATURE:

ADDRESS:

DOCUMENT TYPE:	DATE/TIME NOTARIZED:	DOCUMENT DATE:	FEE CHARGED:

COMMENTS:

RECORD NUMBER: **170**

NOTARY RECORD

FULL NAME:

EMAIL:

THUMB PRINT

PHONE NUMBER:

SIGNER'S SIGNATURE:

ADDRESS:

SERVICES PROVIDED:
- ☐ JURAT
- ☐ OATH
- ☐ ACKNOWLEDGEMENT
- ☐ OTHER : ....

IDENTIFICATION:
- ☐ ID CARD
- ☐ PASSPORT
- ☐ DRIVERS LICENSE
- ☐ OTHER : ....

- ☐ CREDIBLE WITNESS
- ☐ KNOWN PERSONALLY

ID NUMBER:

ISSUED BY:

DATE ISSUE :

EXPIRATION DATE:

WITNESS FULL NAME:

EMAIL:

PHONE NUMBER:

WITNESS SIGNATURE:

ADDRESS:

DOCUMENT TYPE:	DATE/TIME NOTARIZED:	DOCUMENT DATE:	FEE CHARGED:

COMMENTS:

RECORD NUMBER: **171**

NOTARY RECORD

FULL NAME:

EMAIL:

THUMB PRINT

PHONE NUMBER:

SIGNER'S SIGNATURE:

ADDRESS:

SERVICES PROVIDED:
- ☐ JURAT
- ☐ OATH
- ☐ ACKNOWLEDGEMENT
- ☐ OTHER : ....

IDENTIFICATION:
- ☐ ID CARD
- ☐ PASSPORT
- ☐ DRIVERS LICENSE
- ☐ OTHER : ....

- ☐ CREDIBLE WITNESS
- ☐ KNOWN PERSONALLY

ID NUMBER:

ISSUED BY:

DATE ISSUE :

EXPIRATION DATE:

WITNESS FULL NAME:

EMAIL:

PHONE NUMBER:

WITNESS SIGNATURE:

ADDRESS:

DOCUMENT TYPE:	DATE/TIME NOTARIZED:	DOCUMENT DATE:	FEE CHARGED:

COMMENTS:

RECORD NUMBER: **172**

NOTARY RECORD

FULL NAME:

EMAIL:

THUMB PRINT

PHONE NUMBER:

SIGNER'S SIGNATURE:

ADDRESS:

SERVICES PROVIDED:
- ☐ JURAT
- ☐ OATH
- ☐ ACKNOWLEDGEMENT
- ☐ OTHER : ....

IDENTIFICATION:
- ☐ ID CARD
- ☐ PASSPORT
- ☐ DRIVERS LICENSE
- ☐ OTHER : ....

- ☐ CREDIBLE WITNESS
- ☐ KNOWN PERSONALLY

ID NUMBER:

ISSUED BY:

DATE ISSUE :

EXPIRATION DATE:

WITNESS FULL NAME:

EMAIL:

PHONE NUMBER:

WITNESS SIGNATURE:

ADDRESS:

DOCUMENT TYPE:	DATE/TIME NOTARIZED:	DOCUMENT DATE:	FEE CHARGED:

COMMENTS:

RECORD NUMBER: 173

NOTARY RECORD

FULL NAME:

EMAIL:

THUMB PRINT

PHONE NUMBER:

SIGNER'S SIGNATURE:

ADDRESS:

SERVICES PROVIDED:
- ☐ JURAT
- ☐ OATH
- ☐ ACKNOWLEDGEMENT
- ☐ OTHER : ....

IDENTIFICATION:
- ☐ ID CARD
- ☐ PASSPORT
- ☐ DRIVERS LICENSE
- ☐ OTHER : ....

- ☐ CREDIBLE WITNESS
- ☐ KNOWN PERSONALLY

ID NUMBER:

ISSUED BY:

DATE ISSUE :

EXPIRATION DATE:

WITNESS FULL NAME:

EMAIL:

PHONE NUMBER:

WITNESS SIGNATURE:

ADDRESS:

DOCUMENT TYPE:	DATE/TIME NOTARIZED:	DOCUMENT DATE:	FEE CHARGED:

COMMENTS:

RECORD NUMBER: 174

NOTARY RECORD

FULL NAME:	EMAIL:	THUMB PRINT
PHONE NUMBER:	SIGNER'S SIGNATURE:	
ADDRESS:		

SERVICES PROVIDED:	IDENTIFICATION:		ID NUMBER:
☐ JURAT	☐ ID CARD	☐ CREDIBLE WITNESS	
☐ OATH	☐ PASSPORT	☐ KNOWN PERSONALLY	ISSUED BY:
☐ ACKNOWLEDGEMENT	☐ DRIVERS LICENSE		DATE ISSUE : / EXPIRATION DATE:
☐ OTHER :	☐ OTHER :		

WITNESS FULL NAME:	EMAIL:
PHONE NUMBER:	WITNESS SIGNATURE:
ADDRESS:	

DOCUMENT TYPE:	DATE/TIME NOTARIZED:	DOCUMENT DATE:	FEE CHARGED:
COMMENTS:			RECORD NUMBER: **175**

NOTARY RECORD

FULL NAME:	EMAIL:	THUMB PRINT
PHONE NUMBER:	SIGNER'S SIGNATURE:	
ADDRESS:		

SERVICES PROVIDED:	IDENTIFICATION:		ID NUMBER:
☐ JURAT	☐ ID CARD	☐ CREDIBLE WITNESS	
☐ OATH	☐ PASSPORT	☐ KNOWN PERSONALLY	ISSUED BY:
☐ ACKNOWLEDGEMENT	☐ DRIVERS LICENSE		DATE ISSUE : / EXPIRATION DATE:
☐ OTHER :	☐ OTHER :		

WITNESS FULL NAME:	EMAIL:
PHONE NUMBER:	WITNESS SIGNATURE:
ADDRESS:	

DOCUMENT TYPE:	DATE/TIME NOTARIZED:	DOCUMENT DATE:	FEE CHARGED:
COMMENTS:			RECORD NUMBER: **176**

NOTARY RECORD

FULL NAME:

EMAIL:

THUMB PRINT

PHONE NUMBER:

SIGNER'S SIGNATURE:

ADDRESS:

SERVICES PROVIDED:	IDENTIFICATION:		ID NUMBER:
☐ JURAT	☐ ID CARD	☐ CREDIBLE WITNESS	
☐ OATH	☐ PASSPORT	☐ KNOWN PERSONALLY	ISSUED BY:
☐ ACKNOWLEDGEMENT	☐ DRIVERS LICENSE		DATE ISSUE : / EXPIRATION DATE:
☐ OTHER :	☐ OTHER :		

WITNESS FULL NAME:

EMAIL:

PHONE NUMBER:

WITNESS SIGNATURE:

ADDRESS:

DOCUMENT TYPE:	DATE/TIME NOTARIZED:	DOCUMENT DATE:	FEE CHARGED:

COMMENTS:	RECORD NUMBER: **177**

NOTARY RECORD

FULL NAME:

EMAIL:

THUMB PRINT

PHONE NUMBER:

SIGNER'S SIGNATURE:

ADDRESS:

SERVICES PROVIDED:	IDENTIFICATION:		ID NUMBER:
☐ JURAT	☐ ID CARD	☐ CREDIBLE WITNESS	
☐ OATH	☐ PASSPORT	☐ KNOWN PERSONALLY	ISSUED BY:
☐ ACKNOWLEDGEMENT	☐ DRIVERS LICENSE		DATE ISSUE : / EXPIRATION DATE:
☐ OTHER :	☐ OTHER :		

WITNESS FULL NAME:

EMAIL:

PHONE NUMBER:

WITNESS SIGNATURE:

ADDRESS:

DOCUMENT TYPE:	DATE/TIME NOTARIZED:	DOCUMENT DATE:	FEE CHARGED:

COMMENTS:	RECORD NUMBER: **178**

NOTARY RECORD

FULL NAME:	EMAIL:	THUMB PRINT
PHONE NUMBER:	SIGNER'S SIGNATURE:	
ADDRESS:		

SERVICES PROVIDED:	IDENTIFICATION:		ID NUMBER:
☐ JURAT	☐ ID CARD	☐ CREDIBLE WITNESS	
☐ OATH	☐ PASSPORT	☐ KNOWN PERSONALLY	ISSUED BY:
☐ ACKNOWLEDGEMENT	☐ DRIVERS LICENSE		DATE ISSUE : / EXPIRATION DATE:
☐ OTHER :	☐ OTHER :		

WITNESS FULL NAME:	EMAIL:
PHONE NUMBER:	WITNESS SIGNATURE:
ADDRESS:	

DOCUMENT TYPE:	DATE/TIME NOTARIZED:	DOCUMENT DATE:	FEE CHARGED:

COMMENTS:	RECORD NUMBER: **179**

NOTARY RECORD

FULL NAME:	EMAIL:	THUMB PRINT
PHONE NUMBER:	SIGNER'S SIGNATURE:	
ADDRESS:		

SERVICES PROVIDED:	IDENTIFICATION:		ID NUMBER:
☐ JURAT	☐ ID CARD	☐ CREDIBLE WITNESS	
☐ OATH	☐ PASSPORT	☐ KNOWN PERSONALLY	ISSUED BY:
☐ ACKNOWLEDGEMENT	☐ DRIVERS LICENSE		DATE ISSUE : / EXPIRATION DATE:
☐ OTHER :	☐ OTHER :		

WITNESS FULL NAME:	EMAIL:
PHONE NUMBER:	WITNESS SIGNATURE:
ADDRESS:	

DOCUMENT TYPE:	DATE/TIME NOTARIZED:	DOCUMENT DATE:	FEE CHARGED:

COMMENTS:	RECORD NUMBER: **180**

NOTARY RECORD

FULL NAME:	EMAIL:	THUMB PRINT
PHONE NUMBER:	SIGNER'S SIGNATURE:	
ADDRESS:		

SERVICES PROVIDED:	IDENTIFICATION:		ID NUMBER:
☐ JURAT	☐ ID CARD	☐ CREDIBLE WITNESS	
☐ OATH	☐ PASSPORT	☐ KNOWN PERSONALLY	ISSUED BY:
☐ ACKNOWLEDGEMENT	☐ DRIVERS LICENSE		DATE ISSUE : / EXPIRATION DATE:
☐ OTHER :	☐ OTHER :		

WITNESS FULL NAME:	EMAIL:
PHONE NUMBER:	WITNESS SIGNATURE:
ADDRESS:	

DOCUMENT TYPE:	DATE/TIME NOTARIZED:	DOCUMENT DATE:	FEE CHARGED:

COMMENTS:	RECORD NUMBER: **181**

NOTARY RECORD

FULL NAME:	EMAIL:	THUMB PRINT
PHONE NUMBER:	SIGNER'S SIGNATURE:	
ADDRESS:		

SERVICES PROVIDED:	IDENTIFICATION:		ID NUMBER:
☐ JURAT	☐ ID CARD	☐ CREDIBLE WITNESS	
☐ OATH	☐ PASSPORT	☐ KNOWN PERSONALLY	ISSUED BY:
☐ ACKNOWLEDGEMENT	☐ DRIVERS LICENSE		DATE ISSUE : / EXPIRATION DATE:
☐ OTHER :	☐ OTHER :		

WITNESS FULL NAME:	EMAIL:
PHONE NUMBER:	WITNESS SIGNATURE:
ADDRESS:	

DOCUMENT TYPE:	DATE/TIME NOTARIZED:	DOCUMENT DATE:	FEE CHARGED:

COMMENTS:	RECORD NUMBER: **182**

NOTARY RECORD

FULL NAME:

EMAIL:

THUMB PRINT

PHONE NUMBER:

SIGNER'S SIGNATURE:

ADDRESS:

SERVICES PROVIDED:
- ☐ JURAT
- ☐ OATH
- ☐ ACKNOWLEDGEMENT
- ☐ OTHER : ....

IDENTIFICATION:
- ☐ ID CARD
- ☐ PASSPORT
- ☐ DRIVERS LICENSE
- ☐ OTHER : ....

- ☐ CREDIBLE WITNESS
- ☐ KNOWN PERSONALLY

ID NUMBER:

ISSUED BY:

DATE ISSUE :

EXPIRATION DATE:

WITNESS FULL NAME:

EMAIL:

PHONE NUMBER:

WITNESS SIGNATURE:

ADDRESS:

DOCUMENT TYPE:

DATE/TIME NOTARIZED:

DOCUMENT DATE:

FEE CHARGED:

COMMENTS:

RECORD NUMBER: **183**

NOTARY RECORD

FULL NAME:

EMAIL:

THUMB PRINT

PHONE NUMBER:

SIGNER'S SIGNATURE:

ADDRESS:

SERVICES PROVIDED:
- ☐ JURAT
- ☐ OATH
- ☐ ACKNOWLEDGEMENT
- ☐ OTHER : ....

IDENTIFICATION:
- ☐ ID CARD
- ☐ PASSPORT
- ☐ DRIVERS LICENSE
- ☐ OTHER : ....

- ☐ CREDIBLE WITNESS
- ☐ KNOWN PERSONALLY

ID NUMBER:

ISSUED BY:

DATE ISSUE :

EXPIRATION DATE:

WITNESS FULL NAME:

EMAIL:

PHONE NUMBER:

WITNESS SIGNATURE:

ADDRESS:

DOCUMENT TYPE:

DATE/TIME NOTARIZED:

DOCUMENT DATE:

FEE CHARGED:

COMMENTS:

RECORD NUMBER: **184**

NOTARY RECORD

FULL NAME:

EMAIL:

THUMB PRINT

PHONE NUMBER:

SIGNER'S SIGNATURE:

ADDRESS:

SERVICES PROVIDED:
- ☐ JURAT
- ☐ OATH
- ☐ ACKNOWLEDGEMENT
- ☐ OTHER : ....

IDENTIFICATION:
- ☐ ID CARD
- ☐ PASSPORT
- ☐ DRIVERS LICENSE
- ☐ OTHER : ....

- ☐ CREDIBLE WITNESS
- ☐ KNOWN PERSONALLY

ID NUMBER:

ISSUED BY:

DATE ISSUE :

EXPIRATION DATE:

WITNESS FULL NAME:

EMAIL:

PHONE NUMBER:

WITNESS SIGNATURE:

ADDRESS:

DOCUMENT TYPE:	DATE/TIME NOTARIZED:	DOCUMENT DATE:	FEE CHARGED:

COMMENTS:

RECORD NUMBER: **185**

NOTARY RECORD

FULL NAME:

EMAIL:

THUMB PRINT

PHONE NUMBER:

SIGNER'S SIGNATURE:

ADDRESS:

SERVICES PROVIDED:
- ☐ JURAT
- ☐ OATH
- ☐ ACKNOWLEDGEMENT
- ☐ OTHER : ....

IDENTIFICATION:
- ☐ ID CARD
- ☐ PASSPORT
- ☐ DRIVERS LICENSE
- ☐ OTHER : ....

- ☐ CREDIBLE WITNESS
- ☐ KNOWN PERSONALLY

ID NUMBER:

ISSUED BY:

DATE ISSUE :

EXPIRATION DATE:

WITNESS FULL NAME:

EMAIL:

PHONE NUMBER:

WITNESS SIGNATURE:

ADDRESS:

DOCUMENT TYPE:	DATE/TIME NOTARIZED:	DOCUMENT DATE:	FEE CHARGED:

COMMENTS:

RECORD NUMBER: **186**

NOTARY RECORD

FULL NAME:	EMAIL:	THUMB PRINT
PHONE NUMBER:	SIGNER'S SIGNATURE:	
ADDRESS:		

SERVICES PROVIDED:	IDENTIFICATION:		ID NUMBER:
☐ JURAT	☐ ID CARD	☐ CREDIBLE WITNESS	
☐ OATH	☐ PASSPORT	☐ KNOWN PERSONALLY	ISSUED BY:
☐ ACKNOWLEDGEMENT	☐ DRIVERS LICENSE		DATE ISSUE :
☐ OTHER :	☐ OTHER :		EXPIRATION DATE:

WITNESS FULL NAME:	EMAIL:
PHONE NUMBER:	WITNESS SIGNATURE:
ADDRESS:	

DOCUMENT TYPE:	DATE/TIME NOTARIZED:	DOCUMENT DATE:	FEE CHARGED:

COMMENTS:	RECORD NUMBER: 187

NOTARY RECORD

FULL NAME:	EMAIL:	THUMB PRINT
PHONE NUMBER:	SIGNER'S SIGNATURE:	
ADDRESS:		

SERVICES PROVIDED:	IDENTIFICATION:		ID NUMBER:
☐ JURAT	☐ ID CARD	☐ CREDIBLE WITNESS	
☐ OATH	☐ PASSPORT	☐ KNOWN PERSONALLY	ISSUED BY:
☐ ACKNOWLEDGEMENT	☐ DRIVERS LICENSE		DATE ISSUE :
☐ OTHER :	☐ OTHER :		EXPIRATION DATE:

WITNESS FULL NAME:	EMAIL:
PHONE NUMBER:	WITNESS SIGNATURE:
ADDRESS:	

DOCUMENT TYPE:	DATE/TIME NOTARIZED:	DOCUMENT DATE:	FEE CHARGED:

COMMENTS:	RECORD NUMBER: 188

NOTARY RECORD

FULL NAME:

EMAIL:

THUMB PRINT

PHONE NUMBER:

SIGNER'S SIGNATURE:

ADDRESS:

SERVICES PROVIDED:
- ☐ JURAT
- ☐ OATH
- ☐ ACKNOWLEDGEMENT
- ☐ OTHER : ....

IDENTIFICATION:
- ☐ ID CARD
- ☐ PASSPORT
- ☐ DRIVERS LICENSE
- ☐ OTHER : ....

- ☐ CREDIBLE WITNESS
- ☐ KNOWN PERSONALLY

ID NUMBER:

ISSUED BY:

DATE ISSUE :

EXPIRATION DATE:

WITNESS FULL NAME:

EMAIL:

PHONE NUMBER:

WITNESS SIGNATURE:

ADDRESS:

DOCUMENT TYPE:

DATE/TIME NOTARIZED:

DOCUMENT DATE:

FEE CHARGED:

COMMENTS:

RECORD NUMBER: **189**

NOTARY RECORD

FULL NAME:

EMAIL:

THUMB PRINT

PHONE NUMBER:

SIGNER'S SIGNATURE:

ADDRESS:

SERVICES PROVIDED:
- ☐ JURAT
- ☐ OATH
- ☐ ACKNOWLEDGEMENT
- ☐ OTHER : ....

IDENTIFICATION:
- ☐ ID CARD
- ☐ PASSPORT
- ☐ DRIVERS LICENSE
- ☐ OTHER : ....

- ☐ CREDIBLE WITNESS
- ☐ KNOWN PERSONALLY

ID NUMBER:

ISSUED BY:

DATE ISSUE :

EXPIRATION DATE:

WITNESS FULL NAME:

EMAIL:

PHONE NUMBER:

WITNESS SIGNATURE:

ADDRESS:

DOCUMENT TYPE:

DATE/TIME NOTARIZED:

DOCUMENT DATE:

FEE CHARGED:

COMMENTS:

RECORD NUMBER: **190**

NOTARY RECORD

FULL NAME:	EMAIL:	THUMB PRINT
PHONE NUMBER:	SIGNER'S SIGNATURE:	
ADDRESS:		

SERVICES PROVIDED:	IDENTIFICATION:		ID NUMBER:
☐ JURAT	☐ ID CARD	☐ CREDIBLE WITNESS	
☐ OATH	☐ PASSPORT	☐ KNOWN PERSONALLY	ISSUED BY:
☐ ACKNOWLEDGEMENT	☐ DRIVERS LICENSE		DATE ISSUE : / EXPIRATION DATE:
☐ OTHER :	☐ OTHER :		

WITNESS FULL NAME:	EMAIL:
PHONE NUMBER:	WITNESS SIGNATURE:
ADDRESS:	

DOCUMENT TYPE:	DATE/TIME NOTARIZED:	DOCUMENT DATE:	FEE CHARGED:
COMMENTS:			RECORD NUMBER: **191**

NOTARY RECORD

FULL NAME:	EMAIL:	THUMB PRINT
PHONE NUMBER:	SIGNER'S SIGNATURE:	
ADDRESS:		

SERVICES PROVIDED:	IDENTIFICATION:		ID NUMBER:
☐ JURAT	☐ ID CARD	☐ CREDIBLE WITNESS	
☐ OATH	☐ PASSPORT	☐ KNOWN PERSONALLY	ISSUED BY:
☐ ACKNOWLEDGEMENT	☐ DRIVERS LICENSE		DATE ISSUE : / EXPIRATION DATE:
☐ OTHER :	☐ OTHER :		

WITNESS FULL NAME:	EMAIL:
PHONE NUMBER:	WITNESS SIGNATURE:
ADDRESS:	

DOCUMENT TYPE:	DATE/TIME NOTARIZED:	DOCUMENT DATE:	FEE CHARGED:
COMMENTS:			RECORD NUMBER: **192**

NOTARY RECORD

FULL NAME:

EMAIL:

THUMB PRINT

PHONE NUMBER:

SIGNER'S SIGNATURE:

ADDRESS:

SERVICES PROVIDED:	IDENTIFICATION:		ID NUMBER:
☐ JURAT	☐ ID CARD	☐ CREDIBLE WITNESS	
☐ OATH	☐ PASSPORT	☐ KNOWN PERSONALLY	ISSUED BY:
☐ ACKNOWLEDGEMENT	☐ DRIVERS LICENSE		DATE ISSUE : / EXPIRATION DATE:
☐ OTHER :	☐ OTHER :		

WITNESS FULL NAME:

EMAIL:

PHONE NUMBER:

WITNESS SIGNATURE:

ADDRESS:

DOCUMENT TYPE:	DATE/TIME NOTARIZED:	DOCUMENT DATE:	FEE CHARGED:

COMMENTS:	RECORD NUMBER: **193**

NOTARY RECORD

FULL NAME:

EMAIL:

THUMB PRINT

PHONE NUMBER:

SIGNER'S SIGNATURE:

ADDRESS:

SERVICES PROVIDED:	IDENTIFICATION:		ID NUMBER:
☐ JURAT	☐ ID CARD	☐ CREDIBLE WITNESS	
☐ OATH	☐ PASSPORT	☐ KNOWN PERSONALLY	ISSUED BY:
☐ ACKNOWLEDGEMENT	☐ DRIVERS LICENSE		DATE ISSUE : / EXPIRATION DATE:
☐ OTHER :	☐ OTHER :		

WITNESS FULL NAME:

EMAIL:

PHONE NUMBER:

WITNESS SIGNATURE:

ADDRESS:

DOCUMENT TYPE:	DATE/TIME NOTARIZED:	DOCUMENT DATE:	FEE CHARGED:

COMMENTS:	RECORD NUMBER: **194**

NOTARY RECORD

FULL NAME:

EMAIL:

THUMB PRINT

PHONE NUMBER:

SIGNER'S SIGNATURE:

ADDRESS:

SERVICES PROVIDED:
- ☐ JURAT
- ☐ OATH
- ☐ ACKNOWLEDGEMENT
- ☐ OTHER : ....

IDENTIFICATION:
- ☐ ID CARD
- ☐ PASSPORT
- ☐ DRIVERS LICENSE
- ☐ OTHER : ....

- ☐ CREDIBLE WITNESS
- ☐ KNOWN PERSONALLY

ID NUMBER:

ISSUED BY:

DATE ISSUE :

EXPIRATION DATE:

WITNESS FULL NAME:

EMAIL:

PHONE NUMBER:

WITNESS SIGNATURE:

ADDRESS:

DOCUMENT TYPE:	DATE/TIME NOTARIZED:	DOCUMENT DATE:	FEE CHARGED:

COMMENTS:

RECORD NUMBER: **195**

NOTARY RECORD

FULL NAME:

EMAIL:

THUMB PRINT

PHONE NUMBER:

SIGNER'S SIGNATURE:

ADDRESS:

SERVICES PROVIDED:
- ☐ JURAT
- ☐ OATH
- ☐ ACKNOWLEDGEMENT
- ☐ OTHER : ....

IDENTIFICATION:
- ☐ ID CARD
- ☐ PASSPORT
- ☐ DRIVERS LICENSE
- ☐ OTHER : ....

- ☐ CREDIBLE WITNESS
- ☐ KNOWN PERSONALLY

ID NUMBER:

ISSUED BY:

DATE ISSUE :

EXPIRATION DATE:

WITNESS FULL NAME:

EMAIL:

PHONE NUMBER:

WITNESS SIGNATURE:

ADDRESS:

DOCUMENT TYPE:	DATE/TIME NOTARIZED:	DOCUMENT DATE:	FEE CHARGED:

COMMENTS:

RECORD NUMBER: **196**

NOTARY RECORD

FULL NAME:	EMAIL:	THUMB PRINT
PHONE NUMBER:	SIGNER'S SIGNATURE:	
ADDRESS:		

SERVICES PROVIDED:
- ☐ JURAT
- ☐ OATH
- ☐ ACKNOWLEDGEMENT
- ☐ OTHER : ....

IDENTIFICATION:
- ☐ ID CARD
- ☐ PASSPORT
- ☐ DRIVERS LICENSE
- ☐ OTHER : ....
- ☐ CREDIBLE WITNESS
- ☐ KNOWN PERSONALLY

ID NUMBER:

ISSUED BY:

DATE ISSUE :   EXPIRATION DATE:

WITNESS FULL NAME:	EMAIL:
PHONE NUMBER:	WITNESS SIGNATURE:
ADDRESS:	

DOCUMENT TYPE:	DATE/TIME NOTARIZED:	DOCUMENT DATE:	FEE CHARGED:

COMMENTS: RECORD NUMBER: **197**

NOTARY RECORD

FULL NAME:	EMAIL:	THUMB PRINT
PHONE NUMBER:	SIGNER'S SIGNATURE:	
ADDRESS:		

SERVICES PROVIDED:
- ☐ JURAT
- ☐ OATH
- ☐ ACKNOWLEDGEMENT
- ☐ OTHER : ....

IDENTIFICATION:
- ☐ ID CARD
- ☐ PASSPORT
- ☐ DRIVERS LICENSE
- ☐ OTHER : ....
- ☐ CREDIBLE WITNESS
- ☐ KNOWN PERSONALLY

ID NUMBER:

ISSUED BY:

DATE ISSUE :   EXPIRATION DATE:

WITNESS FULL NAME:	EMAIL:
PHONE NUMBER:	WITNESS SIGNATURE:
ADDRESS:	

DOCUMENT TYPE:	DATE/TIME NOTARIZED:	DOCUMENT DATE:	FEE CHARGED:

COMMENTS: RECORD NUMBER: **198**

NOTARY RECORD

FULL NAME:	EMAIL:	THUMB PRINT
PHONE NUMBER:	SIGNER'S SIGNATURE:	
ADDRESS:		

SERVICES PROVIDED:	IDENTIFICATION:		ID NUMBER:
☐ JURAT	☐ ID CARD	☐ CREDIBLE WITNESS	
☐ OATH	☐ PASSPORT	☐ KNOWN PERSONALLY	ISSUED BY:
☐ ACKNOWLEDGEMENT	☐ DRIVERS LICENSE		DATE ISSUE : / EXPIRATION DATE:
☐ OTHER :	☐ OTHER :		

WITNESS FULL NAME:	EMAIL:
PHONE NUMBER:	WITNESS SIGNATURE:
ADDRESS:	

DOCUMENT TYPE:	DATE/TIME NOTARIZED:	DOCUMENT DATE:	FEE CHARGED:

COMMENTS:	RECORD NUMBER: **199**

NOTARY RECORD

FULL NAME:	EMAIL:	THUMB PRINT
PHONE NUMBER:	SIGNER'S SIGNATURE:	
ADDRESS:		

SERVICES PROVIDED:	IDENTIFICATION:		ID NUMBER:
☐ JURAT	☐ ID CARD	☐ CREDIBLE WITNESS	
☐ OATH	☐ PASSPORT	☐ KNOWN PERSONALLY	ISSUED BY:
☐ ACKNOWLEDGEMENT	☐ DRIVERS LICENSE		DATE ISSUE : / EXPIRATION DATE:
☐ OTHER :	☐ OTHER :		

WITNESS FULL NAME:	EMAIL:
PHONE NUMBER:	WITNESS SIGNATURE:
ADDRESS:	

DOCUMENT TYPE:	DATE/TIME NOTARIZED:	DOCUMENT DATE:	FEE CHARGED:

COMMENTS:	RECORD NUMBER: **200**

Made in the USA
Monee, IL
03 April 2024

56278163R00057